SCOTS
IN THE
USA AND CANADA
1825–1875

DISCARD

by
David Dobson

Printed for
Clearfield Company, Inc. by
Genealogical Publishing Co., Inc.
Baltimore, Maryland
1998

Reprinted for
Clearfield Company, Inc. by
Genealogical Publishing Co., Inc.
Baltimore, Maryland
2000

International Standard Book Number: 0-8063-4828-3

Made in the United States of America

INTRODUCTION

Emigration from Scotland to the United States and Canada during the nineteenth century was significant both in absolute and relative terms. The mass movement that occurred was a continuation of a process that had its roots in the seventeenth century. What made Scottish emigrants different from most European emigrants of the Victorian period was the fact that they generally had industrial and commercial skills that were in demand at home and were not rural workers surplus to the needs of an agrarian society. There were notable exceptions to this generalisation particularly those who emigrated during the Highland Clearances. The majority of Scottish emigrants of the period were skilled, educated, workers from urban industrial backgrounds whose expertise was in great demand in the rapidly industrialising cities of North America. The level of annual emigration reflected the fluctuations of the trade cycle during the century.

The number of Scots emigrating is difficult to estimate with accuracy as Irish and latterly Continental emigrants often sailed from Scottish ports while some Scots went via England or Ireland. Between 1825 and 1838 over 60,000 emigrants left Scotland bound for North America; from 1840 to 1853 nearly 30,000 emigrated there; and in 1881 alone 38,000 left for the USA and 3,000 left for Canada, mostly via Greenock. UK statistics only provide overall numbers but US Passenger Arrival Records provide much useful detail.

Genealogists require very specific detail. This compilation is overwhelmingly based on information found in Scots newspapers together with a handful of entries based on documents in the SRO and the USNA. This is part one of an on-going series listing Scots in the USA and Canada.

David Dobson
St Andrews, Scotland. 1998

REFERENCES

Archives

SRO		Scottish Record Office
	B	Burgh Records
	HD	Highland Destitution Papers
	NRAS	Natl. Reg.Archives,Scotland
	RD	Register of Deeds
	RS	Register of Sasines
	SC	Sheriff Court Records
USNA		United States National Archives
	PAR	Passenger Arrival Records

Publications

AJ	Aberdeen Journal
CM	Caledonian Mercury
DJ	Dunfermline Journal
DPCA	Dundee, Perth, Cupar Advertiser
EEC	Edinburgh Evening Courant
EFR	East of Fife Record
F	Fasti Ecclesiae Scoticanae
FA	Fife Advertiser
FFP	Fife Free Press
FH	Fife Herald
FJ	Fife Journal
KCA	King's College, Aberdeen
MCA	Marischal College, Aberdeen
RGU	Roll of Graduates of the University of Glasgow, 1727-1897. W.I.Addison. {Glasgow, 1898}
SG	Scottish Guardian
W	Witness

SCOTS IN USA AND CANADA
1825-1875

ABERNETHY, ALEXANDER DALZIEL, born 1812, third son of
Alexander Abernethy a printer in Edinburgh, died in
Richmond, Virginia, 28.6.1851. [W#1244]

ADAMSON, THOMAS, from Halbeath, Fife, died in St Mary's, Elk
County, Pennsylvania, 30.6.1883. [DJ]

AIKMAN, JAMES, son of James Aikman, High Street, Edinburgh,
died in Charleston, South Carolina, 20.2.1841. [EEC#20192]

AIKMAN, JOHN, in New York, 1831. [SRO.RD5.435.207]

AINSLIE, JOHN, of Marpoffle, an advocate, died in Boonsville,
Missouri, 13.6.1844. [AJ#5039][EEC#21066][W#5.488]

AITCHISON, AMELIA, daughter of John Aitchison in Skerling, wife
of Reverend John M.McGregor, died in Hammond, USA,
4.1.1857. [EEC#23006]

AITCHISON, JAMES M., in Canada 1836. [SRO.RD5.560.442]

AITKEN, HUGH, second son of John Aitken in Ayr, died in Quebec
1.11.1839. [SG#827]

AITKEN, ISABELLA CAROLINE, youngest daughter of Reverend
Roger Aitken, late rector of St John's, Lunenburg, Nova
Scotia, formerly of Aberdeen, died in Fredericton, New
Brunswick, 14.1.1848. [AJ#5223]

ALLAN, ANDREW, married Isabella Anne Smith, daughter of John
Smith, in Montreal 8.9.1848. [SG#1756]

ALLAN, CHRISTIAN, born 1824, wife of William Martin late of
Craigrothie, Fife, died in Buffalo, New York, 5.1.1872.[PJ]

ALLAN, DAVID, born 1837, son of Wilson Allan in Dunfermline,
Fife, a mail conductor, died in Montreal 9.4.1854. [DJ]

ALLAN, JOHN, son of George Allan from Townhill, Dunfermline,
Fife, died at Beechtree, Jefferson County, Pennsylvania,
1886. [DJ, 3.7.1886]

ALLAN, JOHN, from Crossgates, Fife, died in Indiana 16.8.1888.
[DJ]

ALLAN, JOHN, born 1827, from Townhill, Dunfermline, Fife, died
in Knightsville, Indiana, 19.11.1897. [DJ]

ALLAN, WILSON B., born in Dunfermline, Fife, 1797, a collector, died in Montreal 19.5.1872. [PJ]

ALLAN, ..., daughter of George William Allan, born in Moss Park, Toronto, 2.3.1859. [CM#21688]

ALLAN, ..., daughter of George Allan, from Townhill, Dunfermline, Fife, born in Reynoldsville, Jefferson County, Pennsylvania, 10.9.1883. [DJ]

ALLANSHAW, JAMES, born in Berwick-on-Tweed 1792, settled in New Brunswick for 30 years, a merchant and magistrate, died in St Andrews, New Brunswick, 1844. [W#5.457]

ALLISTER, CATHERINE, daughter of William Allister in Beveridgewells, Fife, died in Greenville, Connecticut, 9.9.1870. [DP]

ALLISTER, ISABELLA, born 1806, relict of Andrew Hoggan, died in Rockville, Connecticut, 30.4.1877. [DJ]

ANDERSON, ANDREW, from Auchtermuchty, Fife, died in Sheffield, Iowa, 23.3.1888. [PJ]

ANDERSON, Reverend DAVID, born 1785, late of Boghole, Scotland, died in Philadelphia 8.11.1841. [AJ#4902]

ANDERSON, EDMOND, in South Carolina, 1850. [SRO.RD5.865.191]

ANDERSON, GEORGE, born in Kincardine on Forth 1820, a merchant who settled in Guelph 1856, died in Harrison, Ontario, 26.12.1890. [FFP]

ANDERSON, HENRY R., married Elizabeth G. S. Diaper, daughter of Henry Diaper, in New York 20.10.1859. [EEC#23452]

ANDERSON, JAMES, late of the Scottish Insurance Company in Edinburgh, died in Montreal 13.5.1833. [AJ#4460]

ANDERSON, JAMES, born 1815, former parochial teacher in Carnbee, Fife, died in Ontario, California, 3.4.1899. [DJ]

ANDERSON, JANET, born 1763, relict of Matthew MacFarlane a farmer in Neilston, Renfrewshire, died in Broadlie, Ramsay, Upper Canada, 15.9.1844. [W#5.514]

ANDERSON, JOHN DAVID, born 1819, of HM Naval Works, eldest son of John David Anderson in Burntisland, Fife, died on Ireland Island, Bermuda, 31.7.1857. [FJ]

ANDERSON, ..., daughter of James Anderson, born in Sydney, Cape Breton, 20.2.1847. [AJ#5183]

ANDERSON, JAMES, infant son of James Anderson jr., died in Sydney, Cape Breton, 15.1.1849. [AJ#5277]

ANDERSON, JOHN, in Miramachi, New Brunswick, married Mary
    Garrow, daughter of John Garrow a manufacturer, and relict
    of Alexander Barclay late of Elgin Academy, Morayshire, in
    Aberdeen 22.4.1831. [AJ#4368]

ANDERSON, Dr JOHN, son of John Anderson the Collector of
    Excise in Perth, died at Oak Ridges, Richmond Hill, Toronto,
    19.11.1843. [EEC#20987]

ANDERSON, MARION WATT, daughter of John and Margaret
    Anderson in Pollockshaws, Glasgow, married F.W.Watkin in
    1877, settled in Ontario. [SRO.NRAS.00396.TD230]

ANDERSON, MARY, daughter of John Anderson in Old Aberdeen,
    married John Steven Holmwood in Woolwich, Upper
    Canada, 14.3.1837. [AJ#4660]

ANDERSON, MARY CATHERINE, eldest daughter of Major
    Anderson, HEICS, of Montrave, Fife, married William
    Dickenson, Deputy Inspector General, in Toronto 5.5.1859.
    [CM#21740]

ANDERSON, ROBERT, youngest son of Dr James Anderson of
    Mounie, died in Georgina, Upper Canada, 15.5.1840.
    [EEC#20100]

ANDERSON, or STRACHAN, SUSAN, in Backwynd, Forfar,
    Angus, later in Central Park, Chicago, Illinois, 5.2.1875.
    [SRO.RS.Forfar#30/166]

ANDERSON, ..., son of Captain William Cochrane Anderson of
    the Royal Artillery, died in St Helen's, Upper Canada,
    21.6.1831. [EEC#18678]

ANDERSON, ..., daughter of John Anderson from Edinburgh,
    born in New York 13.1.1839. [SG#742]

ANDREW, Mrs ELIZA, born 1806 in Keith, Banffshire, wife of John
    Andrew a clothier, emigrated via Aberdeen to Quebec
    27.8.1842, settled in Brockville 27.10.1842, died there
    5.12.1842. [AJ#4959]

ANGUS, GEORGE, born 1830, son of John Angus and Mary Scott
    {died 1873} in Cupar, Fife, died in America 4.1869. [FH]

ANGUS, ROBERT, born 1810, a merchant from Angus Place,
    Cupar, Fife, died in Hamilton, Canada, 10.3.1885. [FH]

ANSTRUTHER, CHRISTIAN, born 1768, widow of James
    Ramsay, Edinburgh, died at the residence of her son Hew
    Ramsay in Montreal 9.12.1850. [W#1189]

ARCHIBALD, ANNIE, born 1844, wife of Frank Davis, from
    Dunfermline, Fife, died in Portage, Pennsylvania, 4.1.1907.
    [DJ]

ARMOUR, ANDREW H., Montreal, died in Toronto 19.5.1859.
[CM#21750]

ARMOUR, JOHN, married Margaret, eldest daughter of John
Fisher, in Montreal 14.3.1849.
[AJ#5289][EEC#21808][SG#1818]

ARMOUR, ROBERT, jr., born 1807, advocate for the Province of
Lower Canada, law clerk and clerk of the Committee of the
Legislative Council of Canada, died in Montreal 4.10.1845.
[EEC#21262][W#620]

ARNOLD, Mrs JENNET, born 1748, married Mathew Arnold in
1763, settled in Nova Scotia, died in Truro, Nova Scotia,
5.3.1843. [AJ#4973]

ARNOLD, ..., son of Dr Edmund Arnold, born in Yonkers, New
York, 1856. [EEC#21067]

ARNOT, ANDREW, a stonecutter from Crossgates, Fife, married
Annie Cowan, fourth daughter of John Cowan in Forfar, in
Newark, New Jersey, 11.9.1872. [FFP]

ARNOTT, EDWARD, born in Dunfermline, Fife, 1807, died at
Warehouse Point, Connecticut, 18.8.1870. [FH]

ARNOTT, JOHN, in Canada, 1849. [SRO.RD5.829.549]

ARROL, WILLIAM, eldest son of William Arrol of Butts,
Renfrewshire, married Susannah Jane Burt, eldest daughter
of Darius Burt of Harwich, in Harwich, Upper Canada,
30.7.1849. [SG#1862]

ARTHUR, BARBARA, eldest daughter of James Arthur, King
Street, Old Aberdeen, married Alexander Smith, Annapolis
County, Nova Scotia, in Halifax, Nova Scotia, 28.6.1848.
[AJ#5246]

AULD, JAMES WARDROP, third son of Patrick Auld, died in New
York 6.9.1844. [AJ#5050]

AULDJO, EWERETTA JANE, daughter of George Auldjo, married
Edward Alexander Prentice, in Montreal 23.12.1856.
[EEC#22998]

AULDJO, GEORGE, born 1790, died in Montreal 11.4.1846.
[AJ#5132]

BAIRD, DAVID, from Saltcoats, Ayrshire, a merchant, married
Margaret Boyd, youngest daughter of John Boyd, at St
John's, Newfoundland, 23.8.1849. [SG#1861]

BALD, MAGGIE GIBSON, youngest daughter of John Bald in
Dunfermline, Fife, married John McMillan, in Halifax, Nova
Scotia, 1.6.1870. [FH]

BALFOUR, ALICE, eldest daughter of James Balfour in Letham, Fife, married E.N.Lamont, literary editor of the *Chicago Inter-Ocean*, in New York 5.6.1875. [PJ]

BALFOUR, JAMES BOWER, Lieutenant of HMS Tartar, second son of Francis Balfour of Fernie Castle, Fife, married Martha Maria Emerson, second daughter of G.H.Emerson, QC, Virginia Waters, St John's, Newfoundland, 9.8.1859. [EEC#23414][CM#21827]

BALFOUR, JANE, daughter of Alexander Balfour in Kirkcaldy, Fife, married George Elder jr. a merchant in Montreal, in Boston 2.8.1845. [W#603]

BALFOUR, Dr LEWIS, of Eldrid, Pennsylvania, eldest son of John Balfour, Inspector General of Hospitals in Leven, Fife, married Elizabeth Josephine Hunt Thoms, daughter of N. Thoms in Angelica, New York, in Olcan, New York, 30.9.1880, died in Elrid 27.12.1894. [FFP]

BALFOUR, PETER, born 1819 in Craigrothie, Fife, settled in Hamilton, Ontario, died 1.1897. [FH, 10.2.1897]

BALLANTINE, SUSAN BUIST, daughter of Charles Buist in Burntisland, Fife, died in Charleston, South Carolina, 19.4.1847. [EEC#21504]

BALLINGALL, CHARLOTTE, born 1795, daughter of Alexander Ballingall in Burnmill, Fife, widow of Alexander Sime, died in Dubuque, Iowa, 30.11.1878. [EFR]

BALLINGALL, PATRICK, barrister and city attorney, son of David Ballingall, MA, Rector of Ayr Academy, died in Chicago 21.11.1858. [CM#21618]

BAPTY, MARGARET, born in Roxburghshire, died in Montreal 24.3.1857. [EEC#21078]

BARCLAY, GEORGE, master of the William Ewing of St John's, died in St John's 15.8.1833. [AJ#4471]

BARNET, GEORGE, from Aberdeen, died in Lockport, Will County, Illinois, 5.1.1861. [AJ#5913]

BARNETT, ISABELLA, daughter of James Barnett a merchant tailor in Leven, Fife, married Charles B. Owler 10.4.1846 in Andover, Massachusetts, settled in Charlestown, Boston, 1862. [FH, 28.4.1896]

BARNETT, JAMES, born 1820, son of James Barnett a merchant tailor in Leven, Fife, died in Danvers, Massachusetts, 30.7.1888. [FFP]

BARNETT, LEWIS, born in Aberdeenshire 1773, died in Lochport, Illinois, 1856. [SM#20952]

BARNETT, THOMAS, from Leven, Fife, died in Indianapolis
2.9.1871. [FFP]

BARNETT, THOMAS, born 1825, youngest son of James Barnett
a merchant tailor in Leven, Fife, emigrated to USA 1845,
died in Haverhill, Massachusetts, 22.2.1885. [FFP]

BARNETT, WILLIAM, born 1818, a tinplate and sheetmetal
worker, second son of James Barnett a merchant tailor in
Leven, Fife, emigrated to USA 1845, died in Andover,
Massachusetts, 9.12.1884. [FFP]

BARRIE, Reverend WILLIAM, born in Gateside, Fife, educated at
the University of St Andrews, emigrated to Canada, pastor of
Eramosa congregation in Bon Accord 1843-1877, died in
Guelph, Ontario, 1879. [FA, 16.8.1879]

BATLEY, Miss MARY, late of Glamis, Angus, died in Toronto
9.9.1849. [EEC#21879]

BAULD, EBENEZER HENDERSON, born 1832 in Dunfermline,
Fife, settled in Canada 1861, a minister and a chemist in
Ontario, died in Toronto 24.11.1891. [DJ]

BAXTER, ALEXANDER, an engineer from Milesmark, married
Jean, daughter of George Fotheringham, Grieve Street,
Dunfermline, Fife, in Braddock, Pennsylvania, 17.11.1877.
[DJ]

BEACH, GEORGINA, born 1866, eldest daughter of Joseph
Beach and Helen Butchart from Cupar, Fife, died in
Stockton, California, 3.11.1873. [PJ]

BEATH, ROBERT, born in Dunfermline, Fife, 1821, died in
Beachville, Ontario, 10.1.1895. [FFP]

BEATSON, AGNES JARVIS, daughter of Andrew Beatson, Bridge
Street, Dunfermline, Fife, married James Gillespie, a farmer
in Iowa, at Rockford, Illinois, 7.5.1884. She died in Winthrop,
Iowa, 5.12.1886. [DJ]

BEATTIE, ELIZABETH HARVEY, daughter of Alexander Beattie
MA of the Royal Academy in Tain, Ross-shire, married
Robert Ridley, a merchant, at Peterborough, Upper Canada,
12.5.1842. [AJ#4928]

BEATTIE, ELIZA HARVEY, born 1818, second daughter of
Alexander Beattie MA of the Royal Tain Academy, Ross-
shire, wife of John McNabb, died in Peterboro, Canada
West, 15.7.1862. [AJ#5979]

BEATTIE, JOHN, born 1809, youngest son of Dr Beattie in Insch,
Aberdeenshire, died in Aurora, Wisconsin Territory,
28.3.1839. [AJ#4766]

BEATTIE, WILLIAM, born 1838, son of James Beattie in Benwells,
Old Deer, Aberdeenshire, a stonecutter, died in St Louis,
USA, 15.8.1876. [W#6714]

BELCHES, Mrs MARGARET, sister of Colonel Donald McLeod of
St Kilda, died in Cincinatti, Ohio, 13.8.1835. [AJ#4602]

BELL, ALEXANDER, born 1827, a baker from Dunfermline, Fife,
eldest son of Robert Bell in Gardnersland, Dunfermline, died
at Barclay Mains, USA, 3.10.1872. [FH]

BELL, ANN, wife of Captain William Gordon, late of Greenock,
Renfrewshire, died in Toronto 29.7.1849. [SG#1851]

BELL, ANN, born 1802, daughter of John Bell in Cupar, Fife,
widow of Allen B. Combe, died at the home of her son in law
Charles L. Holt in New York 14.2.1884. [PJ]

BELL, CATHERINE, born 1817, daughter of John Bell a
manufacturer in Cupar, Fife, married William Roy in New
Orleans 17.11.1851. [FJ#990]; she died there 27.5.1858.
[FH]

BELL, SARAH, daughter of William Bell in Toronto, married
Watson Groundwater, in Toronto 14.11.1861. [AJ#5943]

BELL, WILLIAM, a merchant of the House of Livingston, Kinkead
and Company, married Marion Benbow, both of Great Salt
Lake City, Utah Territory, 24.3.1856. [CM#20851]

BENNET, GEORGE, Customs Controller, died in St John's,
Newfoundland, 19.12.1861. [AJ#5949]

BERRY, JAMES ANDERSON, died in Hoboken, New York,
13.5.1852. [W#1337]

BETHUNE, P., from Buckhaven, Fife, emigrated to USA 3.1879.
[PJ, 15.3.1879]

BETHUNE, ROGER HENRY, Hanover, Canada West, married
Jane Frances Ewart, eldest daughter of James Bell Ewart,
Dundas, Canada West, in Toronto 23.1.1862. [EEC#23685]

BETHUNE, W. MACDONALD, born in Ross-shire, a Customs
collector, married Sarah Edwards Channing, eldest daughter
of Thomas Channing, JP, merchant there, in Carbona,
Newfoundland, 1.6.1848. [AJ#5245][SG#1733]

BEVERIDGE, Mrs JESSIE, born 1822, from Leven, Fife, died at
the home of her son-in-law Alexander Thomson in Jersey
City, New Jersey, 30.5.1898. [FFP]

BEVERIDGE, ROBINA, born 1845, married Alexander Thomson
from Leven, Fife, died at 287 West 12 Street, New York,
6.7.1881. [FFP]

BINNY, CHARLES, of the Royal Engineers, married Emma Louise, daughter of J.T.Walford late of the 64th Regiment, in Halifax, Nova Scotia, 27.11.1845. [AJ#5112][EEC#21284]

BIRD, JAMES, born 1773, late Chief Factor of the Hudson Bay Company, died at the Red River Settlement 18.10.1856. [EEC#20993]

BIRNIE, WALTER, born in Aberdeen, a cooper in Quebec for 26 years, died in Quebec 19.9.1849. [AJ#5312]

BIRRELL, DAVID, born in Cupar, Fife, died in Toledo, Ohio, 23.6.1857. [FH]

BIRRELL, GEORGE, born 1810, son of Andrew Birrell a baker in Auchtermuchty, Fife, died in Kinsman, Trumball County, Ohio, 6.9.1861. [FH]

BIRRELL, MAGDALENE, youngest daughter of David Birrell from Cupar, Fife, married John Lambie, in Detroit 13.9.1871. [FH]

BISSETT, ISABELLA, wife of Adam Thomson of the *Montreal Settler*, died in Montreal 2.7.1834. [AJ#4521]

BLACK, CHARLES, second son of James Black, Woodlands, Glasgow, died in Sacramento City, California, 1852. [W#1338]

BLACK, Reverend DAVID, in La Prairie, Lower Canada, married Eliza, daughter of Major Hitterick, in Montreal 13.6.1838. [AJ#4728]

BLACK, ISABELLA, infant daughter of Peter Black from East Wemyss, Fife, died in New York 7.4.1858. [FA]

BLACK, JAMES, formerly of Sinclairtown, Kirkcaldy, Fife, died at St Joseph, Florida, 1842. [FJ:16.6.1842]

BLACK, JAMES, late of Philadelphia, died at 1 East Claremont Street, Edinburgh, 24.3.1843. [EEC#20585]

BLACK, JAMES LEISHMAN, eldest son of Alexander Black, Halifax, Nova Scotia, died at Corstorphine House 26.8.1845. [EEC#21234]

BLACK, JAMES, born 1860, an engineer, eldest son of Andrew Black a cooper from Anstruther, Fife, was killed on the Grand Trunk Railway at Brookville near Lake Ontario, Canada, 21.9.1883. [FJ: 18.10.1883]

BLACK, JOHN, born in Glasgow, of the firm of Watson, Black, and Company, died in Montreal 10.8.1841. [AJ#4888]

BLACK, SAMUEL, to the Indian country in the service of Sir Alexander Mackenzie 1802, joined the North West Company 1805, died on the Columbia River 1841. [AJ#4897]

BLACK, THOMAS, youngest son of William Black a merchant in
    Edinburgh, drowned in the wreck of the Bristol off New York
    21.11.1836. [DPCA#1800]

BLACK, THOMAS, late in Aberdour, Fife, died in Cleveland, Ohio,
    3.11.1882. [DJ]

BLACK, WILLIAM, born in Fraserburgh, Aberdeenshire, died in
    Montreal 26.6.1833. [AJ#4465]

BLACKADDER, FRANCIS, a merchant in Montreal, married
    Margaret Pringle Drummond, third daughter of George
    Drummond, 6 Scotland Street, Edinburgh, in Montreal
    31.12.1844. [W#543]

BLACKBURN, Mrs E.M., in America 1836. [SRO.RD5.553.625]

BLACKIE, ALEXANDER, born 1818, from Tarvit Mill, Fife, died in
    Chicago 28.3.1901. [FH]

BLACKLOCK, THOMAS, in Vermont, 1.11.1860.
    [SRO.RS.Annan#11/6]

BLACKWOOD, JOHN, youngest son of .... Blackwood of the
    Customs in Edinburgh, died on passage to Quebec
    12.7.1831. [EEC#18705]

BLAIR, ARCHIBALD, in Upper Canada, 1836. [SRO.RD5.559.41]

BLAIR, DUGALD, MD, from Greenock, Renfrewshire, died in St
    Stephen, New Brunswick, 23.1.1856. [CM#20699]

BLAIR, AUGUSTUS, former Captain of the 5th Fusiliers, youngest
    son of Colonel Blair of Blair, Ayrshire, died in Hamborough,
    Upper Canada, 1857. [EEC#23070]

BLAKE, JOSEPH, born in Scotland 1795, a farmer, arrived in
    Boston, Charlestown District, USA, late 1821 on the brig
    Missionary, Captain Sears. [USNA]

BLAND, MARY, wife of Reverend John Smith, died in Kingston,
    Upper Canada, 23.2.1834. [SG#232]

BLYTH, MARGARET, or Rollo, born 1813, from Newtown, Cupar,
    Fife, died at her grandson's George Rollo, Lumsden,
    Grenville, Connecticut, 12.1.1895. [PJ]

BOAG, FREDERICK, son of Captain Boag RN, Hamilton, Canada
    West, married Margaret Dalrymple Scott, daughter of Robert
    Scott, St Andrews, Fife, in Beechwood, Victoria, 22.2.1855.
    [EEC#22744]

BOGIE, WILLIAM, from Kirkcaldy, Fife, died in Cincinatti, Ohio,
    15.10.1832. [FH:16.12.1832]

BONNELLA, ANN, wife of William Baillie, youngest daughter of
    John Baillie a farmer in Springfield, Fife, died at Leaden
    Creek, Anderson County, Kansas, 19.9.1869. [PJ]

BONNER, GEORGE WILLIAM GRAHAM, from Colinsburgh, Fife, but in New York, married Margaret Cary Wotherington, daughter of John R. Wotherington of Cooperstown, New York, there 5.10.1881. [EFR]

BONTHRON, JAMES, a baker from Buckhaven, Fife, emigrated to Canada 1855. [FA, 26.5.1855]

BONTHRON, MARGARET, eldest daughter of James Bonthron from Buckhaven, Fife, married Erskine Nicol, in Warrensville, Canada West, 14.1.1858. [FA]

BONTHRON, THOMAS, born 1830, son of John Bonthron in Buckhaven, Fife, died in Southampton, Ontario, 13.4.1891. [PJ]

BONTHRON, ..., daughter of Thomas Bonthron from Buckhaven, Fife, born in Rogerville, Canada West, 5.12.1860. [EFR]

BONTHRON, WILLIAM, born 1842, eldest son of James Bonthron from Buckhaven, Fife, died in Rogerville, Hay County, Canada West, 8.3.1868. [FH]

BORROWMAN, ALEXANDER, in Canada 1848. [SRO.RD5.813.264]

BOULTON, JAMES, Barrister at Law at Niagara, married Margaret Melina Fortie, third daughter of Major Fortie, and niece of Sir Colin Campbell late Lieutenant Governor of Nova Scotia, in Toronto 18.5.1843. [AJ#4980]

BOWIE, MARGARET, daughter of William Bowie in Ayr, relict of Major Robert Henderson of the 78th Highlanders, died in Kemptville, Upper Canada, 6.9.1847. [AJ#5207][EEC#21568]

BOYACK, MARGARET ARNOTT, daughter of Alexander Boyack, Morningside, Edinburgh, married Reverend John Munro of the Free Church, Wallace, at the residence of Reverend Professor King in Halifax, Nova Scotia, 15.10.1852. [W#1381]

BOYCE, JOSEPH, an engineer in New York, 8.6.1870. [SRO.RS.Kinghorn#3/138]

BOYD, ANNA MARIA, eldest daughter of Dr John Boyd of the Army Medical Staff, wife of Chief Justice Jarvis, died in Charlottetown, Prince Edward Island, 28.8.1841. [AJ#4895][EEC#20278]

BOYD, GEORGE HAY, born 1858, son of James Tower Boyd of the Bank of Montreal, died in Brantford, Canada West, 11.9.1861. [AJ#5934]

BOYD, JANE, relict of Dr John Boyd of the Army Medical Staff, died in St John, New Brunswick, 1.2.1842. [EEC#20351]

BOYD, ..., son of James Tower Boyd of the Bank of Montreal, born 22.10.1862 in Brantford, Canada West. [AJ#5992]

BRAND, ELIZABETH H., daughter of William M. Brand, married Elisha N. Warfield, in Lexington, Kentucky, 15.10.1846. [AJ#5159]

BRAND, Mrs GEORGE, from Aberdeen, died in Lexington, Kentucky, 5.9.1849. [AJ#5313]

BRAND, WILLIAM M., born 1803, a planter and manufacturer, son of John Brand a manufacturer in Dundee, died in Lexington, Kentucky, 22.11.1845. [AJ#5113]

BRANDER, JOHN, born in Cairney, Aberdeenshire, 1812, late of Alexandria, Virginia, died in Baltimore 24.1.1850. [AJ#5332]

BROADFOOT, ALEXANDER, Ardrie, Kirkbean, died in Burnside, Port Hope, Toronto, 22.4.1851. [W#1231]

BREWSTER, MARGARET KEY, daughter of Reverend George Brewster in Scoonie, Fife, widow of Joseph Carrier MD, died in New York 10.4.1885. [FJ]

BRODIE, DAVID, a draper, second son of John Brodie in Cupar, Fife, died in Chicago 24.7.1870. [FH]

BRODIE, Mrs ELIZABETH, in New York, 1832. [SRO.RD5.472.34]

BRODIE, ELIZABETH CHALLEN, born 1840, daughter of Dr Hugh Brodie and grand-daughter of Captain Hugh Brodie of the Royal Veterans, died in Cincinatti, USA, 30.4.1849. [SG#1823]

BRODIE, JAMES, from Cupar, Fife, died in Dixon, Illinois, 5.5.1856. [FH]

BROWN, ANDREW, born 1789, a joiner from Crail, Fife, emigrated to America 1830, settled in Natchez, died there 28.1.1871.[EFR]

BROWN, GEORGE, in Toronto, married Anne Nelson, eldest daughter of Thomas Nelson a publisher in Edinburgh, there 17.11.1862. [AJ#5995]

BROWN, GEORGE, born in Wemyss, Fife, 1852, son of John Brown a bootmaker, died at Russell's Hotel, Texas, 2.6.1886. [PJ, 26.6.1886]

BROWN, JOHN, from Netherway, Dumfriesshire, died in Richmond, Virginia, 25.12.1822. [DPCA#1072]

BROWN, JOHN, a joiner from Leven, Fife, died in Hartfield, Connecticut, 15.3.1886. [FFP]

BROWN, JOHN, born 1856, a blacksmith from Leven, Fife, died in Hartfield, Connecticut, 18.9.1891. [FFP]

BROWN, JOHN MOORE, fourth son of Dr W.L.Brown the Principal of Marischal College, Aberdeen, died in Hamilton, Upper Canada, 19.8.1849. [AJ#5307][SG#1858]

BROWN, JUDITH PIGOT, wife of William Robinson, Assistant Commissary General, relict of Francis William Nichol in Tobago, died in St John, Newfoundland, 18.5.1846. [AJ#5142]

BROWN, MARY, daughter of James Brown in Baltimore, niece of O.M.Brown in Cupar, Fife, married William Lisle, a dry goods clerk, in Milwaukee, Wisconsin, 4.5.1857. [PJ]

BROWN, ROBERT, born 1767, formerly of Perth Nurseries, died in Philadelphia 20.9.1845. [EEC#21257][W#616]

BROWN, ROBERT PITT, third son of Robert Brown of New Hall, died in Hamilton, Canada West, 4.12.1850. [EEC#22063][FJ#940][W#1180]

BROWN, WILLIAM, and his wife Ann Guthrie, late of Ardmuddle, Aberdeenshire, died in Brownsville, Illinois, 1.7.1849. [AJ#5299]

BROWN, WILLIAM, a joiner, son of James Brown and Janet Gardiner in Leven, Fife, married Jessie Readie Forbes, third daughter of William Forbes in Dysart, Fife, in Buffalo, New York, 25.8.1857. [PJ]

BROWNING, MARY ANN, wife of James Jackson, late of Glasgow, died in Dumfries, Upper Canada, 7.10.1838. [SG#721]

BRUCE, ARTHUR, born 1761, from Greenock, Renfrewshire, died in Geneva, USA, 5.10.1843. [SG#1240]

BRUCE, JOHN PURVIS, infant son of Thomas Purvis Bruce in Mississippi, died at 1 Queensferry Street, Edinburgh, 11.5.1857. [EEC#21100]

BRUCE, WILLIAM, in New York, 1849. [SRO.RD5.841.683]

BRUNTON, ELIZA, eldest daughter of John Brunton a shipmaster in Aberdeen, married Ronald C. Macfie, London, Canada West, in Boston, USA, 3.11.1862. [AJ#5993]

BRYSON, ROBERT, from Cupar, Fife, married Mary McDonald, daughter of H.E.McDonald of Lyn, in Lyn, Ontario, 4.12.1883. [FH]

BUCHAN, CHARLES, jr., Flamboro East, married Agnes, eldest daughter of John Black, in Guelph, Upper Canada, 5.4.1839. [EEC#19910]

BUCHANAN, ALEXANDER, died in Richmond, Virginia, 4.1833. [SG#175]

BUCHANAN, DRUMMOND, late a Lieutenant of the 90th Foot, died in St Therese, Terrebane County, Canada, 27.7.1849. [AJ#5303]

BUCHANAN, MARY, in New York, 1827. [SRO.RD5.341.296]

BUCHANAN, WILLIAM, a staff assistant surgeon, son of D. Buchanan, Scotland Street, Edinburgh, died in St George's, Bermuda, 27.6.1839. [EEC#119939]

BUCHANAN, ..., son of Isaac Buchanan, born in Toronto 7.5.1844. [W#5.479]

BUCHANAN, ..., son of Isaac Buchanan, born in New York, 29.2.1848. [SG#1702]

BUIST, GEORGE, former manager of the Cupar Gas Works, Fife, died in Halifax, Nova Scotia, 2.11.1879. [PJ]

BURCHHILL, N.R., born in Scotland 1800, a farmer, arrived in Boston, Charlestown District, USA, on the ship Cherub, Captain Shepherd late 1821. [USNA]

BURFORD, W.R.F., in Canada, 1830, [SRO.RD5.421.205]

BURGESS, COLIN, born in Dingwall, Ross-shire, 1797, died in Toronto, Upper Canada, 19.1.1841. [AJ#4866]

BURN, DAVID, late a merchant in Fisherrow, Edinburgh, died in Cherokee, Hamilton, Upper Canada, 2.3.1840. [EEC#20045]

BURN, DAVID, in Canada, 1848. [SRO.RD5.813.399]

BURN, JAMES, born 1783, eldest son of William Burn a merchant in Edinburgh, died in Baltimore 2.10.1832. [EEC#18874][FH#557]

BURN, WILLIAM, in Canada, 1848. [SRO.RD5.813.399]

BURNETT, JAMES G., of Friendville, Aberdeen, married Mary Grace, youngest daughter of Nathan Tyrel of Providence, Rhode Island, in New York 1837. [AJ#4683]

BURNS, ALEXANDER, second son of Alexander Burns in Grangemouth, West Lothian, married Sarah Gairns, youngest daughter of Andrew Gairns from Cupar, Fife, in Chicago 5.1859. [FH]

BURNS, ANN LOCKHART, born 1772, relict of James Darsie, died in Alleghany City, USA, 2.1.1847. [EEC#21463]

BURNS, D., born in Scotland 1793, a clergyman, arrived in Boston, Charlestown District, USA, late 1821 on the schooner Victory, Captain Leavet. [USNA]

BURNS, GEORGE, of Linnbank, born 1790, from Hamilton, Lanarkshire, died in Granville County, North Carolina, 1843. [EEC#20982][W#5.427]

BURNS, ..., son of William Hamilton Burns, barrister at law, born at Isabella Street, Toronto, 12.1.1862. [EEC#23681]

BUSHE, ..., daughter of Mrs Bushe {nee Noel, born in New York
9.11.1830. [EEC#18603]

BUYERS, ELIZABETH, born 1818, wife of George Hay a farmer,
died in Carrick, Bruce County, Canada West, 10.11.1859.
[CM#21904]

CAMERON, Major ANGUS, born 1761, late of Kinlochleven,
Inverness-shire, died in Seymour, Montreal, Upper Canada,
23.8.1847. [AJ#5203][EEC#21556]

CAMERON, ANGUS, in Drumboy in the district of Lochalsh and
Plockton in Wester Ross, to emigrate to America c.1850.
[SRO.HD21/53]

CAMERON, DONALD MHOR, born in Glen Moyl, Inverness-shire,
his wife Ann McLean, and their son Euan Dhu Cameron,
died at Point Fortune, Canada, 7.1832. [AJ#4422]

CAMERON, DUNCAN, born 1774, late Lieutenant Colonel of the
79th Highlanders, died in Toronto 14.10.1842. [AJ#4950]

CAMERON, E.F., in New York, married Elizabeth Campbell,
youngest daughter of Duncan Campbell, in Glasgow
7.12.1859. [CM#21908]

CAMERON, JAMES, MD, born in Kinross 1785, died at 18 North
Moore Street, New York, 12.12.1851. [W#1291]

CAMERON, JOHN, commission merchant in New York, son of
Margaret Webster or Cameron in Dundee, 1857.
[SRO.SC20.34.32.82/87]

CAMERON, MARY ANN, wife of Thomas Campbell late of the
79th Highlanders, died in Canada 27.7.1832. [AJ#4422]

CAMPBELL, Reverend ALEXANDER, a Free Church missionary
in Nova Scotia, married Catherine, eldest daughter of
Alexander Clyne in Scarmalet, at Bower, Caithness,
8.9.1845. [W#610]

CAMPBELL, ARCHIBALD, from Glasgow, married Grace Victoria
Gibson, youngest daughter of John Gibson, in New York
15.11.1849. [SG#1879]

CAMPBELL COLIN, late High Sheriff of Charlotte County, New
Brunswick, died in St Andrew's, New Brunswick, 30.8.1843.
[AJ#4998]

CAMPBELL, GEORGE, a farmer in Chautague County, New York,
26.4.1843. [SRO.RS.Wigtown#3/277, etc]

CAMPBELL, JAMES, in North America,1850. [SRO.RD5.867.346]

CAMPBELL, Reverend JAMES, born 1782, for 22 years minister
of Kildonan in the presbytery of Dornoch, died in Pictou,
Nova Scotia, 7.9.1859. [CM#21861]

CAMPBELL, JANE, third daughter of Colonel Campbell, married
Captain Townsend, Royal Artillery, in Montreal 7.11.1844.
[W#5.524]

CAMPBELL, JOHN, an engineer from Strathbungo, Glasgow,
married Christine Thomson, youngest daughter of Andrew
Thomson from Leven, Fife, in Chicago 24.4.1884. [FFP]

CAMPBELL, ..., daughter of Lieutenant Colonel Sir John
Campbell of the 38th Regiment, born in Halifax, Nova
Scotia, 24.9.1849. [SG#1863]

CAMPBELL, MARY ANNE, youngest daughter of John Campbell
of Carbrook, married Edward T. Renaud a merchant, in
Montreal 1.5.1844. [AJ#5030][EEC#20040][W#5.470]

CAMPBELL, MATTHEW, son of Matthew Campbell in Wigtown,
died in Guelph, Upper Canada, 25.10.1849. [EEC#211891]

CAMPBELL, WILLIAM, died in New Jersey 31.7.1850.
[W#XI.1142]

CAMPBELL, WILLIAM, youngest son of William Campbell of
Queenshill, died in Philadelphia 22.6.1842. [EEC#20393]

CAMPBELL, Lady, widow of Hon. Sir William Campbell the former
Chief Justice and President of the Executive and Legislative
Councils of Upper Canada, died in Toronto 15.2.1843.
[AJ#4967]

CAMPBELL, ..., daughter of Sir John Campbell, Lieutenant
Colonel of the 38th Regiment, born in Halifax, Nova Scotia,
24.9.1849. [EEC#21873]

CARDNO, JANE, wife of William Smith late of the Mill of
Auchnagatt, New Deer, Aberdeenshire, died in Clinton,
Upper Canada, 10.10.1862. [AJ#5993]

CARR, CATHERINE P., born in Scotland 1791, arrived in New
York on the ship Camillas, Captain Peck, 1821. [USNA]

CARRICK, ROBERT, in America, 1837. [SRO.RD5]

CARRINGTON, ISURA, born 1810, daughter of E. Carrington in
Oswego, New York, wife of John Macfarlane, died in
Kingston, Upper Canada, 10.11.1838. [SG#723]

CARRY, Reverend JAMES, Leeds, Megantic County, Lower
Canada, married Grace Matilda Fleming relict of James
Edgar, in Hatly, Lower Canada, 5.6.1851. [W#1244]

CARSWELL, JOHN, from Ceres, Fife, died in Chicago 5.1.1870.
[FJ]

CARTER, JAMES, son of David Carter a wright in Aberdeen,
educated at Marischal College, Aberdeen, 1831-1836,
graduated MA, later a banker and a merchant in St Louis
and Chicago. [MCA.II#478]

CARY, ELIZABETH C., daughter of T.G.Cary, married Louis Agassix, Professor at Harvard College, in New York 25.4.1850. [W#1109]

CASSELS, RICHARD SCOUGALL, youngest son of Walter Gibson Cassels of Blackford House, Edinburgh, married Jessie Thomson, second daughter of John Thomson of Westfield, in Quebec 3.11.1851. [W#1277]

CASSIE, JOHN, from Aberdeen, educated at King's College, Aberdeen, graduated MA 3.1827, later a minister in Port Hope, Canada. [KCA#285]

CATTENACH, JAMES, sr., from Woodend of Finzean, Birse, Aberdeenshire, died in Fergus, Canada West, 5.1.1861. [AJ#5901]

CATTENACH, JOHN, born in Inverness-shire, late Captain of the 92nd Highlanders, fought in the Peninsular War, died in Woodhouse, Upper Canada, 18.8.1852. [W#1368]

CHALMERS, DAVID, The Bend, Woolwich, Canada West, married Aurelia, eldest daughter of B. Bowman Bevis, in Woolwich, Canada West, 8.4.1845. [AJ#5080]

CHALMERS, DAVID, born 1837, from Cupar, Fife, and Edinburgh, late of the *American News Company*, died at 194 Spring Street, New York, 4.2.1886. [FH]

CHALMERS, JOHN, at 2028 Morgan Street, St Louis, Missouri, 1883. [SRO.B9.8.1.283/286]

CHALMERS, PETER, a farmer in Plains, youngest son of Peter Chalmers, died in Trio, Texas, 25.4.1879. [FH]

CHAPLIN, GEORGE, born 1829, from Burntisland, Fife, died at Pine River, Bruce County, Ontario, 4.9.1891. [PJ]

CHARLES, MATTHEW, in Hitchenbrook, Montreal, married Hannah, younger daughter of Peter McKeich in Port Glasgow, 21.7.1831. [AJ#4366]

CHARTERS, MARY JANE, only daughter of Thomas Charters in Roxburghshire, married Alexander Jardine a merchant in St John, New Brunswick, there 19.8.1845. [W#609]

CHEYNE, EUPHEMIA, born 1788, youngest daughter of Alexander Cheyne in Aberdeen, wife of James Johnston, late of Glasgow, died on Waverley Farm, Stanford township, Drummondville, Upper Canada, 10.9.1838. [AJ#4737][SG#714]

CHIENE, JAMES M.M., youngest son of Patrick Chiene, Abercromby Place, Edinburgh, died in Boston 28.9.1857. [EEC#21236]

CHILLAS, DAVID, third son of Robert Chillas in Paisley,
Renfrewshire, died in New York 21.8.1843. [SG#1243]

CHISHOLM, The, of Erdless Castle, married Annie Cecilia
Macdonell, youngest daughter of Angus Macdonell,
granddaughter of Captain Charles Macdonell in Montreal, at
Vienna, Canada West, 1861. [AJ#5945]

CHISHOLM, DAVID, born in Altopkin, Nigg, Ross-shire, Editor of
the *Montreal Gazette*, died in Montreal 1842. [AJ#4949]

CHISHOLM, GEORGE, born 1743, settled in Canada 1769, died
in East Flamborough, Canada, 1843. [AJ#4967]

CHISHOLM, LEWIS, born in Inverness-shire 1770, died in
Montreal 26.6.1847. [AJ#5197]

CHRISTIE, BETSY, wife of Henry Christie, third daughter of
George Christie at the Mains of Lindores, Fife, died in
Chelsea, Massachusetts, 14.2.1859. [FH]

CHRISTIE, JOHN, son of Alexander Christie in Foodie, Fife, died
in Wheaton, Illinois, 30.12.1882. [FH]

CHRISTY, JAMES, from Kildrummy, Aberdeenshire, educated at
King's College, Aberdeen, graduated MA 3.1846, later a
missionary in Canada. [KCA#298]

CHRISTIE, PETER CRICHTON, infant son of Reverend James
Christie, died in Wallace, Nova Scotia, 24.2.1862. [AJ#5959]

CHRISTIE, ..., son of Reverend James Christie, minister of
Wallace, born in Pictou, Nova Scotia, 5.10.1861. [AJ#5940]

CHRISTIE, WILLIAM, eldest son of John Christie of the Royal
Hotel, St Andrews, died in Minnesota Territory 8.5.1852.
[FJ#1018]

CLARK, AMELIA, daughter of Lieutenant Colonel Clark in
Aberdeen, married John Ogilvy Moffatt eldest son of Hon.
George Moffatt, in Montreal 6.8.1844. [AJ#5045]

CLARK, JAMES, in Gloucester, Bytown, Upper Canada, son of
James Clark of Westfield, 1846. [SRO.SC20.34.24.242/243]

CLARKE, JEANNIE, born 1818, wife of William Mackay engineer
of the Margaret of Halifax, died in Halifax, Nova Scotia,
6.12.1847. [SG#1679]

CLARK, MARY B., eldest daughter of Robert Clark a surgeon at
Fort Augustus, Inverness-shire, married Alexander Stewart
McLennan, in Montreal 1.10.1859. [CM#21869]

CLEGHORN, ARCHIBALD, late a merchant in Leith, Midlothian,
died in New Glasgow, Canada, 25.9.1840. [EEC#20126]

CLEGHORN, JAMES, in Montreal 1836. [SRO.RD5.548.475]

CLEGHORN, Captain JAMES, born Cupar, Fife, 1833, master of
the J.P.Taylor, died in Chicago 5.12.1868. [FJ]

CLEGHORN, WILLIAM, late a merchant in Leith, Midlothian, died in New Glasgow, near Montreal, 26.5.1849. [EEC#21835]

CLEGHORN, Mrs, in Canada, 1849. [SRO.RD5.835.42]

CLELAND, JAMES, born in Glasgow 1812, a printer, died in Toronto 25.1.1857. [EEC#21030]

CLEPHANE, GEORGE, eldest son of Andrew Clephane the Sheriff of Fife, died in Fergus, Canada, 2.5.1851. [FJ#962][W#1225]

CLIMIE, JOHN M., of Innisfil, married Jean Hay, eldest daughter of Robert Hay formerly a farmer in Cossins, Angus, at Bowmanville, Canada West, 24.1.1855. [EEC.22711]

COCHRAN, A.W., married Magdalene, youngest daughter of James Kerr, in Quebec 24.7.1843. [EEC#20648]

COCHRANE, ROBERT, born in Kirkcudbright, 'many years resident in New York', died in Albany, USA, 30.7.1849. [SG#1847]

COCHRANE, SAMUEL, born in Kirkcudbright 1805, a merchant in New York, died near there 31.8.1859. [CM#21838]

COLQUHOUN, JOHN, from Paisley, Renfrewshire, in Rhode Island 1844. [SRO.GD1.814.6]

COMBE, ALLAN, born 1792, a blacksmith from Cupar, Fife, died in New York 7.7.1851. [FH]

CONNELL, WILLIAM, brother of Dr Connell, was drowned in the wreck of the Mamlouk on his passage home from America 9.1847. [SG#1718]

CONNING, WILLIAM, in New York, 13.5.1822. [SRO.RS.Whithorn#1/208,211]

CONSTABLE, JOHN, in Toronto, son of Alexander Constable a farmer in Craigsanquhar, 1857. [SRO.SC20.34.32.67/69]

COOPER, ALEXANDER, second son of James Cooper an upholsterer in Edinburgh, died in New York 8.1832. [EEC#18868]

COLQUHOUN, THOMAS, late of Gilmourholm, died in Petersburg, Virginia, 1832. [AJ#4399]

COULL, GEORGE, from Rathven, educated at King's College, Aberdeen, graduated MA 3.1850, later minister of Smyrna, Canada. [KCA#302]

COUSIN, WILLIAM, a farmer in American Park City, Utah, 14.6.1876. [SRO.RS.Dysart#5/278]

COWAN, ANDREW, a merchant in Montreal, married Mary, second daughter of Hew Aiken, in Newtown on Ayr 1.4.1839. [EEC#19881]

COWAN, WILLIAM, a builder from Colinsburgh, Fife, died in Hamilton, Upper Canada, 18.3 1841. [FH]

COWIE, JOHN, surgeon of the Hudson Bay Company, married Margaret Heddell, third daughter of James Greig of Sandsound, in Lerwick, Shetland Islands, 21.5.1839. [EEC#19904]

CRABB, WILLIAM, born in Leven, Fife, emigrated to USA 1870, settled in Lowell, Massachusetts, then in Newark, New Jersey, did 19.5.1890. [FH, 25.6.1890]

CRAIG, DAVID, West 31 Street, New York, 13.5.1854. [SRO.RS.Auchtermuchty#5/8]

CRAIG,......, son of D.J.Craig, born in Montreal 2.8.1859. [CM#21809]

CRAWFORD, JAMES, assistant surgeon of the 24th Regiment, married Emma Matilda Platt, daughter of George Platt, in Montreal 1834. [AJ#4512]

CRAWFORD, PETER, son of Peter Crawford in Barbieston, Ayrshire, died in New York 5.9.1843. [SG#1239]

CREIGHTON, or KIRKPATRICK, MARY, in America, 4.3.1867. [SRO.RS.Lochmaben#6/213]

CRITNAN, G.W., born in Scotland 1787, a farmer, arrived in Boston, Charlestown District, USA, late 1821 on the schooner <u>Victory</u>, Captain Leavet. [USNA]

CROMBIE, JOHN, born 1832, brother of James Crombie postmaster of Ladybank, Fife, died in New York 11.12.1871. [FH]

CROMBIE, ..., son of David Crombie, born in Hamilton, Canada West, 4.9.1859. [CM#21850]

CROSS, ..., son of Reverend John Cross, born 20.5.1845 in Blairsville, Pennsylvania. [AJ#5088]

CRUDEN, EUPHEMIA BUCHAN, daughter of Reverend George Cruden, Logie Buchan, Aberdeen, married Charles R. Ross of the Commercial Bank of Toronto, at Glenlogie, Kingston, Canada, 13.5.1843. [AJ#4979]

CRUICKSHANK, JOHN, born 1791, son of Dr Cruickshank of Forgie, Aberdeenshire, died in Toronto 20.8.1850. [AJ#5363]

CRUICKSHANK, JOHN, HELEN AND JEAN, the three eldest children of John Cruickshank blacksmith in Tulloch, Meldrum, Aberdeenshire, died on the <u>St Lawrence</u> at the quarantine station of Quebec 14.9.1848. [AJ#5263]

CUMMING, HANNAH, late of Dandaleith, Rothes, Morayshire, married Alexander Grant from Pittsburgh, in Kingston, Canada, 3.11.1835. [AJ#4589]

CUNNINGHAM, ELIZABETH, born 1860, daughter of Peter
Hannay Cunningham of Pittairthie, Fife, died in Washington,
DC, 24.2.1862. [EEC#23692]

CUNNINGHAM, JOHN,, born in Scotland 1781, a laborer, arrived
in New York on the ship Camillas, Captain Peck, 1821.
[USNA]

CUNNINGHAM, JOHN, from Renton, Dunbartonshire, died in
Streetsville, Hamilton, Canada West, 8.3.1857. [EEC#2106]

CUNNINGHAME, WILLIAM JOHN, of Lorn House, Lieutenant of
the 42nd Royal Highlanders, died in Halifax, Nova Scotia,
21.6.1850. [AJ#5350][W#XI.1133]

CUNNINGHAM, WILLIAM MOUAT, born 1658, second son of
Peter Hannay Cunningham of Pittairthie, Fife, died in
Washington, DC, 28.2.1862. [EEC#23694]

CUNYNGHAME, FREDERICK ALEXANDER, younger son of Sir
William Augustus Cunynghame of Milncraig, died in York,
Upper Canada, 10.4.1842. [EEC#20374]

CURR, EMILIA, born 1833, from Cupar, Fife, wife of James
Simpson an engineer, died in Brockville, Ontario, 5.1.1893.
[PJ]

CURRIE, GEORGE, born in Scotland 1799, a laborer, arrived in
New York 1821 on the ship Camillas, Captain Peck. [USNA]

CURRIE, GEORGE, second son of William Currie in Greenland,
Roxburghshire, died in New Orleans 1.1829. [EEC#18655]

DALGETTY, or CAMPBELL, JANE, in Caldhame, Forfar, Angus,
then in Soloman City, Kansas, 27.6.1871.
[SRO.RS.Forfar#26/163, etc]

DALGLEISH, WILLIAM, from Tinnygask, Saline, Fife, died in
Binbrook, Canada West, 17.9.1868. [DP]

DALLAS, MARGARET JOHNSTON, eldest daughter of James
Dallas, Orillia Cottage, married Reverend Frederick A.
O'Meara, a missionary of the Church of England at Sault
Sainte Marie, Upper Canada, in Orillia, Upper Canada,
25.4.1840. [EEC#20062]

DALTON, ..., son of Captain Charles J. Dalton, Royal Artillery,
born in St John's, New Brunswick, 25.9.1850. [W#XI.1158]

DAVIDSON, AGNES, third daughter of William Davidson a
merchant in Wick, Caithness, married E.S.Babcock a
merchant, at Madison, Indiana, 28.5.1844.
[AJ#5044][EEC#21080]

DAVIDSON, FRANCIS, youngest son of David Davidson, died in
Montreal 22.9.1842. [AJ#4847][EEC#20522]

DAVIDSON, ISABELLA JEMIMA, third daughter of James
Davidson of Burnside, married Absolom Shade in Burnside
of Woolwich, Upper Canada, 16.3.1837. [AJ#4660]

DAVIDSON, ISABELLA, second daughter of William Davidson in
Wick, Caithness, married John Ingle, Evansville, in Madison,
Indiana, 29.11.1842. [AJ#4958]

DAVIDSON, JAMES, born in Edinburgh 1811, a druggist, died in
Cincinatti, USA, 20.12.1856. [EEC#21002]

DAVIDSON, JANET GARDEN, infant daughter of George
Davidson of Springfield, Upper Canada, died in Berlin,
Waterloo, Upper Canada, 19.8.1841. [AJ#4899]

DAVIDSON, JOHN BAYNE, infant son of George Davidson, died
in New Aberdeen, Canada West, 7.9.1848. [AJ#5257]

DAVIDSON, LAWRENCE, WS, married Emma, youngest daughter
of John Pryor of Halifax, Nova Scotia, in Edinburgh
6.12.1831. [AJ#4379]

DAVIDSON, ROBERT, born 1815, second son of William
Davidson a merchant in Wick, Caithness, drowned in the
River Ohio near Louisville, Kentucky, 22.6.1840.
[EEC#20088]

DAVIDSON, ROBERT, born 1833, a former reporter of the
Arbroath Guide, Angus, then sub-editor of the *Scottish
American*, died at the Battle of Bull Run, Virginia, 21.7.1861.
[AJ#5930]

DAVIDSON, THOMAS, born 1817, from Banffshire, died in
Hamilton, Canada West, 8.3.1857. [EEC#21066]

DAVIDSON, WILLIAM, MD, in Madison, Indiana, son of William
Davidson a fishcurer in Wick, Caithness, 1863.
[SRO.SC20.34.46.267/271]

DAVIDSON, ..., son of John A. Davidson, born in Woodburn,
Nichol township, Upper Canada, 20.4.1841. [AJ#4899]

DAVIDSON, ..., son of Charles A. Davidson, born 4.10.1862 at
114 Forsyth Street, New York. [AJ#5992]

DAVNIE, ELIZABETH JANET, from Aberdeen, married James
Law, a merchant in Auburn, in New York 24.7.1838.
[AJ#4730]

DAWSON, RUTH, born 1835, wife of John Greig from Cupar
{1831-1908}, Fife, died in Madison, Wisconsin, 30.3.1910.
[FH]

DAWSON, WILLIAM ALFRED, from Mobile, Alabama, married
Jane, second daughter of Sir William Ogilvy of Carnousie,
Banffshire, in Edinburgh 12.8.1842. [AJ#4936]

DEARIE, MARIA, eldest daughter of Robert Dearie a wine-
merchant in Glasgow, married Henry Heaton Bury from New
York, in Glasgow 1856. [CM#20734]

DEMPSTER, JANE, wife of Samuel Hargreaves, late of Sauchie,
Alloa, died in Providence, Delaware County, Pennsylvania,
1859. [CM#21894]

DEMPSTER, JOHN, a merchant formerly in Greenock,
Renfrewshire, died in Halifax, Nova Scotia, 25.10.1848.
[EEC#21743][SG#1272]

DENHOLM, JOHN, late of Quebec, died in Blythswood 2.1.1831.
[AJ#4334][EEC#188593]

DENNISTOUN, ROBERT, Colgrain, married Maxwell, daughter of
Major Hamilton, late of the 78th Highlanders, in
Peterborough, Upper Canada, 24.12.1839. [EEC#20027]

DEVINE, JAMES, from Aberdeen, educated at King's College,
Aberdeen, graduated MA 3.1840, later a missionary in
Canada. [KCA#293]

DEWAR, ANDREW, born 1835, third son of James Dewar in
Gauldry, Fife, died at the residence of John Cameron, 264
Church Street, Toronto, 3.9.1859. [FH]

DICK, THOMAS, in USA, 1836. [SRO.RD5.552.34]

DICK, WILLIAM, from Kirkcaldy, Fife, died in Canada West 1849.
[FA:21.7.1849]

DICKIE, DAVID, a teacher in USA, married Mary Torrance of 65
Nicolson Street, Edinburgh, youngest daughter of John
Torrance, a manufacturer in Stonehouse, Lanarkshire,
18.11.1839. [EEC#19978]

DICKIE, ROBERT, a farmer late of Auldmains of Kilwinning,
Ayrshire, died in Beverly, Galt, Upper Canada, 10.3.1849.
[SG#1817]

DICKSON, CHARLES RANALDSON, second son of David R.
Dickson of Blairhall, Perthshire, married Fanny, daughter of
J. Macartney a banker in Carlow, in Hamilton, Upper
Canada, 7.1.1843. [AJ#4965][EEC#20554]

DICKSON, DAVID, married Mary Maria Cunningham, eldest
daughter of Dr Charles Cunningham, Grand Island, New
York, at Cedar Creek, Oxford, Upper Canada, 20.10.1837.
[DPCA#1848]

DICKSON, DAVID SOMERVILLE RANALDSON, late of the Scots
Greys, died in Toronto 13.2.1838. [AJ#4709]

DICKSON, EDWARD, from New York, married Isobel, second
daughter of William Gordon, in Montrose, Angus, 16.5.1843.
[AJ#4973]

DICKSON, ..., son of James Gilchrist Dickson, born in Montreal
21.11.1859. [EEC#23452]

DICKSON, ROBERT, of Woodlawn, Niagara, died in Leghorn
27.11.1846. [EEC#21433]

DICKSON, WILLIAM, in Galt, for many years a member of the
Legislative Council of Upper Canada, died in Woodlawn,
Niagara, 19.2.1846. [EEC#21326]

DICKSON, ..., son of David Dickson, born in St Cuthbert's, West
Oxford, Upper Canada, 22.8.1838. [SG#703]

DICKSON, ..., son of David Dickson, born at Lake County,
Indiana, 24.7.1851. [W#1269]

DODS, Dr ROBERT, late of Prora, East Lothian, died in New
Windsor, Maryland, 27.7.1833. [AJ#4471]

DODS, Miss ..., youngest daughter of Mr Dods, Seton Hill, East
Lothian, died at Cote de la Visitation, Montreal, 5.3.1855.
[EEC.22715]

DOIG, THOMAS, an accountant, second son of James Doig a
manufacturer in Dundee, died in Pescadero, Santa Cruz
County, California, 27.11.1863. [EFR]

DONALD, JOHN, Callander, late of St Louis, USA, died at the
residence of his nephew John Blacklock, Invercargill, Otago,
New Zealand, 31.3.1859. [CM#21806]

DONALD, WILLIAM, from Aberdeen, educated at King's College,
Aberdeen, graduated MA 3.1832, a schoolmaster in Huntly,
Aberdeenshire, then a minister in St Johns, New Brunswick.
[KCA#287]

DONALDSON, R.G.F., from Burntisland, Fife, married Isabella
Suttie, second daughter of James Suttie a mason in
Dunshalt, in Denver, Colorado, 8.5.1882. [DJ]

DOTT, ROBERT, born at Chance Inn, Ceres, Fife, 1824,
emigrated to Toronto 1840, a merchant in Illinois, Iowa, and
Dakota, settled in Alexandria, South Dakota, 1885, died
1905. [FH, 3.1.1906]

DOUGLAS, GEORGE, in New York, 1827. [SRO.RD5.330.672]

DOUGLAS, ..., son of George Bruce Douglas from Portobello,
Edinburgh, born in Brooklyn, New York, 17.10.1859.
[CM#21874]

DOUNE, DUNCAN MACRAE, from Bendoloch in the district of
Lochalsh and Plockton, Wester Ross, to emigrate to
America ca.1850. [SRO.HD21/53]

DOW, MARGARET, wife of William Dow, late of Banffshire, died in
Whitby, USA, 1833. [AJ#4482]

DOWNES, HENRY GRANVILLE, medical staff, son of Major
   Charles Downes in Edinburgh, married Annie MacLean
   Leonard, third daughter of Charles E. Leonard, Sydney,
   Cape Breton, there 28.10.1848. [EEC#21738][SG#1770]
DOWNIE, GEORGE HART, son of John Mackay Downie in
   Edinburgh, married Agnes Ranken Wilson, daughter of
   William Wilson in Kilmarnock, Ayrshire, in New York
   25.12.1854. [EEC.22687]
DOWNY, ALEXANDER, born in Scotland 1785, a laborer, arrived
   in Barnstable, USA, late 1821 on the schooner Alert, Captain
   Pease. [USNA]
DRON, MARGARET, born 1805, wife of James Elder from
   Auchtermuchty, Fife, died in Johnsonville, Trumball County,
   Ohio, 21.2.1874. [FH]
DRON, WILLIAM, born 1812 in Auchtermuchty, Fife, emigrated to
   USA 1839, died in Augusta 4.7.1879. [FH:31.7.1879]
DRUMMOND, Reverend JAMES, pastor of the Congregationalist
   Church in Quebec, died in Quebec 1.9.1849. [SG#1860]
DRUMMOND, JANE, daughter of George Drummond a builder in
   Edinburgh, married John Redpath from Montreal, in
   Kingston, Upper Canada, 11.9.1835. [AJ#4581]
DRUMMOND, THOMAS S., in America, 1848.
   [SRO.RD5.804.175]
DRYSDALE, ALICIA MURRAY, youngest daughter of William
   Drysdale in Edinburgh, married Reverend John Stewart, St
   George's Channel, Cape Breton, in Halifax, Nova Scotia,
   22.9.1835. [AJ#4584]
DRYSDALE, ROBERT, a baker in Kirkcaldy, Fife, then in America,
   23.5.1863. [SRO.RS.Kirkcaldy#12/129]
DRYSDALE, ..., son of Alexander Drysdale, born 13.9.1841 in
   Jessiefield, Garafraxa, Canada. [AJ#4894][EEC#20276]
DUFF, ALFRED, born 1833, Royal Navy, died in Upper Canada
   29.11.1857. [EEC#21298]
DUFF, JAMES, a gardener from Montrave, Fife, emigrated to
   America 10.1878. [FH, 17.10.1878]
DUFF, WILLIAM C., born 1781, second son of Reverend William
   Duff in Foveran, Aberdeenshire, died in Amherstburg,
   Canada West, 12.7.1861. [AJ#5928]
DUFFUS, or WYLLIE, JANE, in Erichtbank, Blairgowrie,
   Perthshire, then in Airleywight, Washington, New York,
   28.2.1849. [SRO.RS.Forfar#16/18]

DUNBAR, GEORGE HOME, late Lieutenant of the 93rd
Highlanders, third son of Professor Dunbar of Edinburgh
University, died in Niagara, Upper Canada, 10.1839.
[SG#820]

DUNBAR, ROBERT, born in Ovenstone, Carnbee, Fife, 1812,
emigrated to Canada, settled in Buffalo 1834, founder of the
Eagle Iron Works, died in Buffalo 18.9.1890. [PJ,
11.10.1890]

DUNCAN, ALEXANDER, born 1821 eldest son of Reverend
Alexander Duncan minister of the Associate Congregation of
Original Seceders in Dundee, died in Savannah, USA,
23.9.1842. [AJ#4951]

DUNCAN, CHARLES, born 1831, son of Henry Duncan in Cupar,
Fife, a clothier and housefurnisher, settled in Brantford,
Ontario, married Jeannie Bell, youngest daughter of John
Bell in Sheridac, New Brunswick, 10.8.1858, died in
Brantford 7.10.1907. [FH]

DUNCAN, DAVID, a jeweller late in Montrose, Angus, eldest son
of William Duncan in Cupar, Fife, died in New York
28.9.1877. [FH]

DUNCAN, ..., daughter of David Duncan, born in New York
30.4.1859. [CM#21730]

DUNCAN, JAMES, third son of Henry Duncan in Cupar, Fife, a
watchmaker, died in Knoxville, North America, 20.9.1878.
[FH]

DUNCAN, JESSY SCOTT, born 1831, eldest daughter of
Alexander Duncan in Providence, Rhode Island, died in New
York 24.11.1847. [EEC#21596]

DUNCAN, MARGARET ROBERTSON, second daughter of J.
Duncan in Tullo, Aberdeenshire, married George Nicol,
Brooke, Canada West, there 15.8.1861. [AJ#5933]

DUNCAN, MARY, eldest daughter of William Duncan a tailor in
Cupar, Fife, married John Campbell, in Olympia, California,
12.5.1860. [FH]

DUNCAN, SAMUEL ALEXANDER, infant son of Alexander
Duncan, died in Providence, Rhode Island, 29.12.1845.
[EEC#21300]

DUNCAN, ..., daughter of William Butler Duncan, born in New
York 7.2.1855. [EEC.22706]

DUNCAN, ..., daughter of David Duncan, born in New York
30.4.1859. [EEC#23364]

DUNDAS, WILLIAM, of Ochtertyre, late of the HEICS in Bengal, died at Niagara Falls 20.8.1842. [EEC#20509]

DUNLOP, JAMES, in Petersburg, Virginia, 1830. [SRO.RD5.402.628]

DUNLOP, ROBERT, born 1817, of Dunlop and Tennant, youngest son of Dr Dunlop of Beith, Ayshire, died in Petersburg, Virginia, 1.9.1859. [CM#21846]

DUNLOP, ROBERT GRAHAM, born in Greenock, Renfrewshire, 1790, son of Alexander Dunlop of Keppoch, died in Gairbraid, Goderich, Upper Canada, 28.2.1841. [AJ#4868]

DUNLOP, WILLIAM, a surgeon, third son of Alexander Dunlop of Keppoch, died in Montreal 29.6.1848. [AJ#5246][EEC#21686][SG#1735]

DURIE, CATHERINE, wife of James Gibb late of Caldcots, Fettercairn, Kincardineshire, died at 24 Moss township, London District, Upper Canada, 23.12.1842. [AJ#4981]

DURIE, JAMES, born 1806 in Torryburn, Fife, died in Tremont, Westchester County, New York, 3.10.1870. [FH]

DURNO, JAMES, a watchmaker, son of James Durno in New Deer, Aberdeenshire, died in Philadelphia 2.5.1835. [AJ#4575]

DURNO, Mrs JANE, born 1803, wife of James Durno, late of Aberdeen, died in Upper Alton, Illinois, 21.8.1841. [AJ#4900]

DYCE, CHRISTIAN, eldest daughter of John Dyce in Tillygreig, Aberdeenshire, relict of Robert Allan R.N., died in St John's, New Brunswick, 10.6.1844. [AJ#5036]

DYCE, Reverend ROBERT, Episcopalian clergyman from Drumlithie, Kincardineshire, died in Washington, USA, 1.1842. [AJ#4914]

DYKES, LEONARD J.B., fifth son of J.D.B.Dykes, Dovensby Hall, Cumberland, died in New York 9.1.1844. [EEC#20995]

EDGAR, JAMES, last son of John Edgar of Keithock, Angus, died on passage to Quebec 9.6.1841. [AJ#4883]

EDGAR, JAMES, born 1819, son of James Edgar in Edinburgh, died in Lennoxville, Canada East, 6.4.1850. [W#XI.1106]

EDIE, Mrs ...., from Leslie, Fife, died in Alleghany City, USA, 28.2.1852. [FH:1.4.1852]

EDINBURGH, W.H., in Montreal 1836. [SRO.RD5.550.579]

EDWARD, JAMES, Natchez, married Charlotte Bruen, eldest daughter of James Farrand, New York, in New York 2.9.1839. [EEC#19963]

EDWARDS, JAMES K., from Dundee, educated at King's College, Aberdeen, graduated MA 3.1847, later in Montreal. [KCA#299]

ELDER, JAMES, from Auchtermuchty, Fife, died in Johnston, Trumball County, Ohio, 21.2.1874. [FH]

ELDER, JOHN, born in Crail, Fife, 1806, emigrated to USA 1840, settled in Patterson, New Jersey, died in Hartford City 1898. [EFR, 23.12.1898]

ELLIOT, ANDREW, sr., born in Hawick, Roxburghshire, 1776, died in Crowland, Port Robinson, Toronto, 26.1.1857. [EEC#21042]

ELLIOT, JOHN, born 1803, from Kelso, Roxburghshire, died in Tuscumba, Alabama, 21.9.1839. [EEC#19976]

ESSON, ROBERT, of Napponee, married Jane Anne Stoughton, in Bath, Upper Canada, 15.4.1844. [AJ#5028][EEC#20037]

ELLIOT, THOMAS, born in Westerkirk parish, Dumfries-shire, 1821, died at his brother's house in Galt, Canada, 26.10.1848. [SG#1764]

ESSON, Mrs CHARLES, died at her son's house in Halifax, Nova Scotia, 1843. [AJ#5017]

EWING, Reverend ALEXANDER, eldest son of Alexander Ewing a mathematician in Edinburgh, died in Bermuda 18.10.1822. [DPCA#1068]

EWING, ALEXANDER, born 1846, son of James Lindsay Ewing, died in Mobile 8.2.1849. [AJ#5283][EEC#21792]

FAIRLIE, MARGARET, wife of Robert Fairlie from Greenock, Renfrewshire, died in Naperville, Du Page County, Illinois, 11.9.1844. [SG#1342]

FALCONER, JOHN, from Elgin, Morayshire, a merchant in Baltimore, married Charlotte L. Soutar, daughter of Mr Soutar in Norfolk, Virginia, in Norfolk 8.5.1845. [AJ#5088]

FALCONER, MADELINE, youngest daughter of A. Falconer of Blackhills, Nairn, married John C. Bennet, at Woodstock, Upper Canada, 8.4.1841. [AJ#4870]

FARMER, JEAN, born 1817, daughter of David Farmer in Methilhill, Fife, married William Greig 14.10.1833, emigrated to USA 1850, settled in Detroit, moved to Hastings, Dakota County, Minnesota, 1855, settled in Grafton, Subley County, Minnesota, 1875, died there 24.3.1890. [FH, 23.4.1890]

FARNIE, JAMES, from St Andrews, Fife, then in Canada, 1853. [SRO.B9.8.1.213/116]

FARQUHARSON, JOHN, born 1764 in Knockando, Morayshire, settled in Nova Scotia 1792, died in Dartmouth, Halifax, Nova Scotia, 11.6.1842. [AJ#4931]

FERGUS, JAMES, born in Glasgow 1777, '40 years in Newfoundland', died in St John's, Newfoundland, 4.7.1849. [SG#1850]

FERGUSON, ADAM, an advocate, late of Woodhill, Perthshire, a Member of the Legislative Council of Canada, died in Woodhill, Canada West, 25.9.1862. [AJ#5988]

FERGUSON, AGNES, widow of James Scott Ferguson fifth son of Adam Ferguson of Woodhill, died in Gamonoque, Canada West, 13.3.1852. [W#1319]

FERGUSON, DAVID, civil engineer, third son of James Ferguson in Bathgate, West Lothian, died at Point St Charles, Montreal, 5.4.1859. [CM#21712]

FERGUSON, DAVID, a manufacturer in Kirkcaldy, Fife, later in Waupun, Dodge City, USA, 3.6.1863. [SRO.RS.Kirkcaldy#10/66]

FERGUSON, GEORGE, born 1818, from Ayrshire, then in Roxburgh, Massachusetts, died in Gold Run, California, 17.7.1851. [W#1260]

FERGUSON, HENRY, youngest son of Archibald Ferguson, 22 St James Square, Edinburgh, died in New Orleans 22.10.1859. [CM#21904]

FERGUSON, JAMES, from Texas, married Marie, daughter of Gottfried H. Heslet, in Stuttgart, Germany, 28.10.1848. [EEC#21735]

FERGUSON, JAMES SCOTT, son of Adam Ferguson of Woodhill, died in Woodhill, Canada West, 7.7.1850. [AJ#5352][W#XI.1138]

FERGUSON, JAMES, born in Perthshire 1803, died at Long Point, Quebec, 1.1.1857. [EEC#21042]

FERGUSON, JESSIE, fourth daughter of William Ferguson a farmer in Backmoss of New Deer, Aberdeenshire, married William Jamieson from Oxford township, Kent County, Canada West, at New Deer 10.1861. [AJ#5939]

FERGUSON, JOHN, from Edinburgh, died in Esquesing, Toronto, 28.8.1843. [EEC#20675]

FERGUSON, RONALD CRAWFURD, fourth son of William Ferguson of Kilrie, died in Frederickston, New Brunswick, 18.8.1852. [W#1366]

FERME, JOHN, in America 1838. [SRO.RD5.588.86]

FERRIE, JESSIE EDMONSTONE, youngest daughter of
Reverend William Ferrie of Sydney Street Church, died at St
John's, New Brunswick, 26.9.1852. [FJ#1033][W#1373]

FERRIER, Reverend JOHN, from Auchtermuchty, Fife, died at
Bladon Springs near Mobile, South Carolina, 27.12.1860.
[FH: 14.2.1861]

FERRIER, LOUIS HENRY, of Belleside, HM Customs Collector of
Quebec, died in Marchmont near Quebec 28.1.1833.
[DPCA, 15.3.1833]

FINLAY, JAMES, second son of Robert Finlay a millwright in
Cupar, Fife, died in Baltimore 2.5.1868. [FH]

FINDLAY, ..., son of Robert K. Findlay from Glasgow, born in
Madison, Wisconsin, 31.1.1857. [EEC#21034]

FINLAYSON, ALEXANDER, from Aronisk in the district of
Lochalsh and Plockton, Wester Ross, to emigrate to
America ca.1850. [SRO.HD21/53]

FINLAYSON, DUNCAN, in Ardelvie, in the district of Lochalsh and
Plockton in Wester Ross, to emigrate to America c.1850.
[SRO.HD21/53]

FINLAYSON, DUNCAN, from Aronisk in the district of Lochalsh
and Plockton, Wester Ross, to emigrate to America ca.1850.
[SRO.HD21/53]

FINLAYSON, FINLAY, from Erbusaig in the district of Lochalsh
and Plockton, Wester Ross, to emigrate to America ca.1850.
[SRO.HD21/53]

FINLAYSON, JOHN BAIN, from Erbusaig in the district of
Lochalsh and Plockton, Wester Ross, to emigrate to
America ca.1850. [SRO.HD21/53]

FINLAYSON, JOHN, from Kirkton of Lochalsh in the district of
Lochalsh and Plockton, Wester Ross, to emigrate to
America ca.1850. [SRO.HD21/53]

FINLAYSON, RORY, from Aronisk in the district of Lochalsh and
Plockton, Wester Ross, to emigrate to America ca.1850.
[SRO.HD21/53]

FINNIE, MARY ANN, born in Scotland 1781, with 4 children,
arrived in New York on the ship Camillas, Captain Peck,
1821. [USNA]

FISHER, ANDREW, in Canada 1836. [SRO.RD5.559.1]

FISHER, JANET, wife of James Walker, died in Peterborough,
Canada West, 16.5.1849. [SG#1829]

FISHER, JOHN, born 1805, formerly in Newburgh, Fife, late a
master mariner in Liverpool, died in Ann Arbor, Michigan,
20.2.1851. [FJ#952]

FISHER, JOHN, second son of Alexander Fisher, Lebanon House, Cupar, Fife, died in Madison, Wisconsin, 20.8.1872. [FH]

FISKEN, ..., daughter of John Fisken, born in Toronto 24.1.1848. [SG#1695]

FLEMING, JANET, relict of Hans Fleming in Crail, Fife, died at the residence of his son in Astoria, USA, 1855. [FH, 10.5.1855]

FLEMING, JOHN, born in Aberdeen, President of the Bank of Montreal, died 30.9.1832. [AJ#4422]

FLEMING, MARGARET, born 1812, wife of John Sharp Hall WS, died in Montreal 24.1.1840. [EEC#20044]

FLETCHER, DUNCAN, formerly Captain of the Loyal American Regiment and latterly of the Veterans Battalion in Scotland, died in Culross 12.1.1823. [DPCA#1070]

FLETT, MARGARET, daughter of Robert Flett, from Kirkwall in the Orkney Islands, in Quebec, married James S. Sloane, a printer in Toronto, there 28.1.1857. [EEC#21042]

FORBES, ALEXANDER, late Major of the 79th Highlanders, died in Kingston, Upper Canada, 30.3.1851. [W#1217]

FORBES, ANN, third daughter of James Forbes in Kingland Place, Aberdeen, married Reverend Alexander Gardiner, minister of Fergus, Upper Canada, in Quebec 16.8.1838. [AJ#4731]

FORBES, Mrs E., widow of Robert Melvin a merchant in Aberdeen, married William Tytler of Irvineside, in Fergus township, Upper Canada, 7.3.1837. [AJ#4662]

FORBES, FRANCIS, born 1766, son of Harry Forbes in Aberdeenshire, a master cooper and tavern keeper, emigrated 1792, settled at Longue Point, Canada, died at 2 St Paul Street, Montreal, 23.9.1849. [AJ#5312]

FORBES, FRANCIS, born 1817 son of Sir Charles Forbes, died in San Francisco 30.12.1849. [AJ#5335][W#XI.1099]

FORBES, JAMES MOIR, editor of the *Aberdeen Journal*, married Sarah Jane Robertson, third daughter of George Robertson in Aberdeen, in Quebec 23.10.1838. [AJ#4744]

FORBES, JOHN, from Aberdeen, married Ann Kidd, in Montreal 21.6.1833. [AJ#4464]

FORBES, JOSEPH YEAMAN, born 1853, son of Mr Forbes of Sydney Grammar School, died in North Sydney, Cape Breton, 17.1.1862. [AJ#5954]

FOREMAN, JAMES, in Halifax, 1831. [SRO.RD5.432.226]

FORREST, DAVID, son of John R, Forrest late of George Square, Edinburgh, then in The Walk, Alloa, Clackmannanshire, died in New York 27.10.1859. [EEC#23443][CM#21886]

FORREST, or IRVING, JOANNA, in Prince Edward Island
23.9.1865. [SRO.RS.Annan#12/51]

FORREST, Reverend JOHN, MA {Edinburgh}, minister of the First
Presbyterian Church of Charleston, married Sarah Jane
Keith Ogier, daughter of Thomas Ogier in Charleston, in
Charleston, South Carolina, 7.5.1834. [SG#258]

FORREST, SARAH, daughter of Reverend John Forrest, died in
Charleston, South Carolina, 23.5.1842. [EEC#20390]

FORREST, WILLIAM J., a civil engineer in Canada 6.12.1862.
[SRO.RS.Annan#11/175]

FORREST, ..., son of Reverend John Forrest, born in Charleston,
South Carolina, 13.7.1838. [SG#700]

FORRESTER, DAVID, a wright from Forfar, Angus, later in
Canada 27.10.1826. [SRO.RS.Forfar#7/73]

FORRESTER, ROBERT, married Cynthia Minerva Tilton, second
daughter of A.F.Tilton, Dunville, Illinois, at Montreal
24.4.1849. [SG#1823]

FORSYTH, HELEN, eldest daughter of James Forsyth a baker
from Aberdeen, married Walter Sloan from Penn County,
Pennsylvania, at Mac's Hotel on the Ovens River 29.7.1862.
[AJ#5990]

FORSYTH, JOHN, born 1760, member of the Legislative Council
of Lower Canada, died in Montreal, 27.12.1837.
[DPCA#1849] [AJ#4695]

FRAME, JOHN, a former calico printer in Glasgow, died in
Nottawasaga, Upper Canada, 15.9.1844. [SG#1342]

FRASER, CATHERINE, eldest daughter of Reverend Alexander
Fraser in Inverness, wife of Hugh Denoon of Belleville,
Collector of Customs, died in Pictou, Nova Scotia,
11.11.1838. [SG#735]

FRASER, ELIZA, daughter of Paul Fraser in Pictou, Nova Scotia,
widow of John Lyle a merchant in Halifax, Nova Scotia,
married Robert Lamond a writer in Glasgow, in Edinburgh
3.5.1856. [CM#20808]

FRASER, FANNY MARIA, youngest daughter of Alexander
Garden Fraser in New York, married Reverend John Pirie
from Edinburgh, in Kenmore 12.6.1861. [AJ#5919]

FRASER, Lieutenant Colonel F.A.M., Deputy Quartermaster
General, died in Montreal 28.10.1848.
[AJ#5265][EEC#21743]

FRASER, JAMES, of T. and J. Fraser and Company, Ferry Street,
New York, married Ella Keran, eldest daughter of Andrew
Keran, a merchant in Petersburg, Virginia, in Petersburg
12.5.1859. [CM#21736]

FRASER, JEMIMA JOHNSTONE, daughter of John Fraser of
Farraline, Inverness, died in Toronto 18.9.1848. [SG#1760]

FRASER, JOHN, born 1837, from Inverness, died in New York
15.4.1856. [CM#20784]

FRASER, MARGARET, daughter of James Fraser in Farraline,
Inverness, an advocate, died in Hamilton, Canada West,
23.9.1847. [AJ#5207]

FRASER, REBECCA HARIOT, daughter of John Fraser of
Farraline, advocate in Inverness, married Reverend John
Gray in Toronto 27.8.1850. [AJ#5362]; she died in Kingston,
Canada West 10.2.1851. [FJ#950][W#1200]

FRASER, SIMON, educated at King's College, Aberdeen,
graduated MA 3.1835, later a minister in MacNab, Canada.
[KCA#290]

FREELAND, JOHN, a merchant, married Isabella, daughter of
Henry Rankin, a merchant, in New York 31.7.1839.
[SG#803]

FULLARTON, HELEN, wife of John K. Fullarton of Skeldon, died
in Skeldon, Grand River Ouse, Niagara District, Upper
Canada, 3.9.1841; their son ... born 24.8.1841.
[AJ#4892][EEC#20271]

FULLARTON, PHILIP K., fourth son of William Fullarton of
Skeldon, Ayrshire, died at Port Robinson, Niagara District,
Canada West, 26.1.1848. [SG#1704]

FYFE, WILLIAM, a joiner from Forfar, Angus, later in Albany, New
York, and Florida, 21.1.1880. [SRO.RS.Forfar#37/67]

GAIRNS, WILLIAM, born in Cupar, Fife, married Catherine
McCurrie from Perthshire, in Chicago 23.11.1871. [PJ]

GALBRAITH, JANE SOMES, eldest daughter of Colin Galbraith a
writer in Edinburgh, married James Keith Edwards MA,
editor of the *Montreal Transcript*, on the <u>John Bell</u> in
Montreal 3.8.1859. [EEC#23407][CM#21810]

GALLOWAY, Reverend GEORGE, born in Girthon 1802, minister
of the Presbyterian Church in Bermuda, died there
13.3.1834. [SG#244]

GALLOWAY, Reverend GEORGE, born in Peterhead,
Aberdeenshire, 1816, MA, a minister in Markham, Canada,
for 5 years, died 11.11.1844. [AJ#5059]

GALLOWAY, HECTOR, from Baldinny, Fife, died in Keokuk, USA, 2.1.1861. [FH]

GALLOWAY, THOMAS, born 1833, from Radernie, Fife, died in St Louis 31.1.1877. [FH]

GALT, ..., daughter of John Galt registrar of Huron County, born in Goderich, Upper Canada, 5.8.1844.
[EEC#21094][W#5.506]

GALT, ..., son of Alexander T. Galt, born in Sherbrooke, Canada, 24.5.1850. [W#1124]

GAMBLE, JANE, born in Scotland 1785, with 4 children, arrived in New York on the ship Camillas, Captain Peck, 1821. [USNA]

GANTT, ROBERT, born in Scotland 1799, a merchant, arrived in Savannah, USA, on the ship Pallas, Captain Land, late 1821. [USNA]

GARDEN, ELIZABETH, born 1776, relict of Harry Greig of Fullerton, Angus, died in Montreal 18.4.1848. [AJ#5237]

GARDINER, Reverend ALEXANDER, died in Fergus, Upper Canada, 13.12.1841. [AJ#4906]

GARDNER, JAMES CORBET, eldest son of James Gardner a perfumer in Glasgow, died in Mobile 19.6.1844. [SG#1324]

GARDNER, JAMES OGILVIE, son of James Ogilvie Gardner in Edinburgh, died in Nashville, Tennessee, 2.1847.
[EEC#21496]

GARDNER, MARGARET, daughter of David Gardner a baker in Cupar, Fife,wife of James Duncan, died in Knoxville 23.9.1881. [FH]

GARLAND, ANDREW MELVILLE, infant son of J. Garland from Giffordtown, Fife, died at Portage la Prairie, Manitoba, 3.7.1881. [PJ]

GAUGAIN, JAMES THOMAS, born 1824, son of John James Gaugain in Edinburgh, died in Mexico 1847. [SG#1701]

GAUL, JOHN, born in Scotland 1786, a laborer, arrived in Barnstable, USA, late 1821 on the schooner Alert, Captain Pearse. [USNA]

GEALE, AUGUSTA MARIA, wife of Walter H. Dickson a member of the Legislative Council of Canada, died in Niagara, Canada West, 6.3.1855. [EEC.22719]

GEDDES, ANNIE, second daughter of Robert Geddes in Burntisland, Fife, married Alexander Crichton, at Beamsville, Canada, 23.8.1859. [FA]

GEDDES, MARGARET, wife of Andrew Geddes a merchant in Aberdeen then the Crown Lands agent for the County of Waterloo, died in Elora, Canada West, 12.11.1850. [AJ#5370]

GEIKIE, CAROLINE CATHERINE ELEANORA, daughter of James St. Geikie, St Simon's Island, Georgia, married Jonathan Duncan Gleig, HEICS, in Arbroath, Angus, 5.3.1832. [AJ#4395][FH#525]

GENTLE, ROBERT, once a farmer in Airdrie, Crail, Fife, died in South Carolina 6.7.1882. [EFR]

GIBB, JOSEPH, born 1783, late pastor of the Congregationalist Church in Banff for 20 years, emigrated from Aberdeen to Montreal 14.4.1830, died in Stanstead, Lower Canada, 14.6.1833. [AJ#4465]

GIBB,SARAH, daughter of Thomas Gibb, Millwood, Lanarkshire, married John Wedderspoon, a merchant in San Francisco, California, there 7.6.1859. [CM#21792]

GIBSON, DUNLOP GERARD, youngest son of John Gibson WS in Edinburgh, died in New York 11.4.1835. [AJ#4558]

GIBSON, JAMES, of Ashbrook, RN, third son of Archibald Gibson WS, died in Woodstock, Upper Canada, 21.4.1839. [EEC#19910]

GIBSON, JAMES TAYLOR, late of Linlithgow, West Lothian, of the firm of John Gibson and Company in New Orleans, died there 12.2.1849. [SG#1804]

GIBSON, WILLIAM, a tenter in the Lebanon Works, Cupar, Fife, emigrated to USA 3.1870. [FH, 10.3.1870]

GILCHRIST, MARGARET, wife of Reverend James Williamson the Professor of Natural Philosophy at Queen's College, died in Kingston, Canada, 3.4.1847. [AJ#5187][EEC#21501]

GILCHRIST, WILLIAM, in Tecumseh, Michigan, married Catherine, youngest daughter of William Swan, Queen Anne Street, {Dunfermline?}, in Dunfermline, Fife, 3.2.1846. [EEC#21304]

GILKISON, WILLIAM, late from Glasgow, died in Tuscarora, Upper Canada, 25.4.1833. [SG#146]

GILLESPIE, ALEXANDER, in Toronto, son of George Gillespie in Biggar Park, Lanarkshire, married Maria Holmes, second daughter of Colonel Patterson Royal Artillery, in Woolwich, Upper Canada, 26.12.1843. [AJ#5017][EEC#21001][W#5.439]

GILLESPIE, ..., son of Alexander Gillespie, born in Quebec 9.3.1849. [EEC#21793]

GILLESPIE, ELIZA P., youngest daughter of late David Gillespie in
New York, married Alexander Anderson a colonial surgeon,
in Victoria, Hong Kong, 30.4.1844. [EEC#21087]

GILLESPIE, JAMES, son of George Gillespie of Biggar Park, died
in Canada 27.7.1832. [AJ#4422]

GILLESPIE, ROBERT, born 3.6.1855, son of Robert Gillespie from
Lassodie Colliery, died at Rocky Mountain Mines, Almy,
Utah, 3.3.1881. [FH, 14.4.1881]

GILLESPIE, ..., daughter of Alexander Gillespie, a merchant in
Quebec, born 7.6.1847. [AJ#5191][EEC#21521]

GILMOR, JAMES, son of Allan Gilmor in Eaglesham, died in
Solano County, California, 1881.
[SRO.NRAS#0608.T.book 67]

GILMOR, ..., daughter of J.C.Gilmor, born in Toronto 2.3.1848.
[SG#1703]

GILMOUR, ALLAN, from Glasgow but late of Quebec, married
Agnes, fourth daughter of John Strang of St Andrews, at St
Andrews, New Brunswick, 10.6.1839. [SG#789]

GILMOUR, JOHN, in America, 1836. [SRO.RD5.560.110]

GILMOUR, JOHN, born in Sanquhar, Dumfries-shire, 1837, died in
New York 29.1.1857. [EEC#21042]

GILMOUR, JOHN K., only son of Matthew Gilmour in Glasgow,
died in Newhaven, Connecticut, 17.12.1849. [W#XI.1079]

GIRDWOOD, JOHN, late builder in Kirkintilloch, son of George
Girdwood in Carnwath, Lanarkshire, died in Hamilton,
Canada West 10.12.1856. [EEC#20990]

GLASS, ..., daughter of Reverend C. Gordon Glass, Principal of
Woodstock College, born 25.2.1862 in Woodstock, New
Brunswick, [AJ#5961]

GOODALL, GAVIN, Galt, Canada West, married Janet Ainslie,
daughter of William Ainslie, at Moat near Roslin 20.3.1862.
[EEC#23694]

GOODWILLIE, ROBERT, born 1800 in Aberdour, Fife, died in
Montreal 18.10.1854. [FH]

GORDON, ALEXANDER, born 1765, died in Gilston, Canada
West, 12.10.1849. [AJ#5314][EEC#21886]

GORDON, Major ALEXANDER, late of Mount Dorchester, died in
Niagara, Upper Canada, 12.8.1850. [AJ#5362][W#XI.1155]

GORDON, AUGUSTA, daughter of Alexander Gordon the sheriff
substitute of Sutherland, married James H. Doyle in Toronto,
at Christ Church Cathedral, Montreal, 3.8.1862. [AJ#5982]

GORDON, FRANCIS, Ouseland on the Grand River, died in Paris,
Brandford, Upper Canada, 26.1.1839. [EEC#19919]

GORDON, FRANCIS, born in Huntly, Aberdeenshire, 1781, died in
New York 1.12.1862. [AJ#5998]

GORDON, GEORGE, born 1815, son of Adam Gordon of
Cairnfield, died in Baltimore 1861. [AJ#5904]

GORDON, JOHN, late of Dalcharn, Kildonan, Sutherland, died at
Scotch Hill, Pictou, Nova Scotia, 30.5.1835. [AJ#4572]

GORDON, MARGARET, born 1840, daughter of Charles Gordon
from Peterhead, Aberdeenshire, wife of William Mackenzie
from Kinnethmont, died in Mitchell, Canada West, 8.6.1862.
[AJ#5974]

GORDON, SARAH ELEANOR, third daughter of William Gordon,
married Charles R.A.Routh from New York, in Munbank,
Dumfries, 29.4.1857. [EEC#23046]

GORDON, THOMAS, born in Dumfries, died in Quebec 26.7.1832.
[AJ#4422][EEC#18859]

GORDON, WILLIAM, born in Aberdeen, a fishing tackle maker,
died in Quebec 8.8.1834. [AJ#4523]

GORDON, WILLIAM, born 1810, third son of William Gordon a
vintner in Montrose, Angus, a joiner, died in New Orleans
27.9.1835. [AJ#4587]

GORDON, Captain WILLIAM, late of Greenock, Renfrewshire,
died in Toronto 31.7.1849. [SG#1851]

GORDON, ..., daughter of Leslie Gordon, born in Cookesville,
Ontario, 9.11.1876. [AJ#6727]

GOURLAY, THOMAS, born 1846, second son of Thomas Gourlay
a vintner in Ceres, Fife, died in San Francisco
18.3.1880.[PJ]

GOURLAY, WILLIAM, born 1833 in Ceres, Fife, a mason, died at
132 Strachan Avenue, Toronto, 25.3.1882. [PJ]

GOWANS, JAMES, born in Lanarkshire 1766, emigrated to USA
1821, settled in Indiana, Ohio and Kentucky, died in
Louisville, Kentucky, 22.10.1849. [SG#1877]

GRAHAM, ELSPETH, widow of John Ritchie in Byers of
Balmerino, Fife, died at Home Wood, Beaver County,
Pennsylvania, 23.8.1869. [PJ]

GRAHAM, JANE, wife of Thomas Morland in Montreal, died in
Boston, USA, 13.12.1856. [CM#20987]

GRAHAM, PATRICK, of Robshill, WS in Edinburgh, died in Mobile
11.11.1859. [CM#21894]

GRAHAM, WILLIAM, in USA, 1836. [SRO.RD5.552.110]

GRAHAM, WILLIAM R., in Vaughan, Toronto, 8.11.1855.
[SRO.RS.Annan#10/15]

GRANT, DONALD, born 1798 in Cromdale, Strathspey, late of
Halifax, Nova Scotia, died in Tain 27.4.1848. [AJ#5237]

GRANT, LOUISA, relict of Maximilian Grant of the Royal
Engineers Department, died at Lower Cove, St John, New
Brunswick, 18.5.1857. [EEC#23064]

GRANT, WILLIAM, son of James Grant of Burnhall, WS, married
Miss Barker, daughter of A. Barker of Hallowell Grange,
Prince Edward District, in Picton, Canada West, 1843.
[AJ#5001]

GRANT, ..., daughter of John Grant, surgeon of the 79th
Highlanders, born in the Citadel, Quebec, 25.1.1849.
[AJ#5279]

GRAY, ALEXANDER, born 1779, a farmer from Milltown of
Craigston, King-Edward, Aberdeenshire, died in North
Oxford township, Oxford County, Canada West, 19.12.1860.
[AJ#5897]

GRAY, ANDREW, in America, 1836. [SRO.RD5.560.660]

GRAY, ANNE, youngest daughter of David Gray in Edinburgh,
married William Young, Blantford, Canada West, in Buffalo,
New York, 24.11.1858. [CM#21620]

GRAY, JOHN, born in Scotland 1783, a gentleman, arrived in
Waldboro, USA, on the ship Lydia, Captain Adams, late
1821. [USNA]

GRAY, MARGARET, eldest daughter of W. Gray in Pittinan,
Daviot, Aberdeenshire, married William Singer a farmer in
Garafraxa, at Guelph, Canada West, 8.5.1861. [AJ#5918]

GRAY, ROBERT, late of Edinburgh, an engineer in North
Madison, married Helena Steele, daughter of J.C.Steele, in
Milton, USA, 23.1.1851. [W#1194]

GRAY, MARGARETTA SOPHIA, daughter of William Gray a
printer in Montreal, married James Webster in Aberdeen
26.2.1832. [AJ#4386]

GRAY, WILLIAM M., from Edinburgh, in Buffalo, married Henrietta
A. Perry, eldest daughter of Miles Perry in Auburn, New
York, in Auburn 30.11.1858. [CM#21620]

GREEN, D., late Captain of the Royal Regiment, married Isabella
Hatch, fourth daughter of Harris Hatch, St Andrews, in St
Andrews, New Brunswick, 15.5.1850. [W#XI.1125]

GREENFIELD, WILLIAM, born in Caithness 1765, died in Detroit,
Michigan, 16.1.1845. [AJ#5071]

GREIG, DAVID, attorney and solicitor in New York, eldest son of
Alexander Greig WS, died in New York 10.9.1847.
[EEC#21560]

GREIG, JAMES, engineer in Paterson, near New York, son of
Simon Greig in East Wemyss, Fife, 1853.
[SRO.SC20.34.29.275/278]

GREIG, JOHN W., second son of Alexander Greig WS, died in
New Orleans 7.1.1848. [EEC#21620][SG#1693]

GREIG, JOHN, born in Cupar, Fife, 4.6.1831, son of Thomas
Greig a baker and brewer in Ladywynd, Cupar, a tenant
farmer in Balgarvie, settled in Madison, Wisconsin, 1878,
died there 18.6.1908. [FH, 1.7.1908]

GREIG, JOHNATHAN, conductor of the Cupar Harmonic Society,
Fife, emigrated to California 11.1857. [FJ, 26.11.1857]

GREIG, ROBERT, born in Dunshalt, Fife, emigrated to USA 1854,
died at Wells River, Vermont, 3.5.1881. [PJ]

GREIG, WILLIAM, born in Buckhaven, Fife, 2.6.1807, married
Jean farmer in Methilhill, Fife, 14.10.1833, emigrated to USA
1850, settled in Detroit, moved to Hastings, Dakota County,
Minnesota, 1855, settled in Grafton, Sibley County,
Minnesota, 1875, died there 24.3.1890. [FH, 23.4.1890]

GREIG, ..., son of Reverend Patrick Greig, born in Hamilton,
Canada West, 18.9.1859. [CM#21850]

GRIEVE, ..., son of Walter Grieve, born in St John's,
Newfoundland, 30.4.1848. [EEC#21660]

GRINTON, DAVID, a cabinetmaker from Musselburgh, Midlothian,
died in Morrisiana Village, New York, 24..1859. [CM#21737]

GULLAN, JOHN G., late teacher in Glasgow, died in Montreal
12.1.1845. [W#545]

GULLAN, MARGARET, wife of Hugh Cameron from Glasgow,
died in Hamilton, Canada West, 1.9.1849. [SG#1866]

GUNN, SINCLAIR MANNERS, youngest son of Reverend
Alexander Gunn in Watten, Caithness, died on the <u>George</u>
off the Banks of Newfoundland 2.8.1843. [AJ#4998]

GUTHRIE, PETER, born 1806, from the Mains of Mayen,
Rothiemay, died in St Charles, Kane County, Illinois, 1861.
[AJ#5951]

HACCAU, HARRIET, wife of John McConnell an advocate, died in
Markbroom, Canandagua, New York, 29.7.1833. [SG#173]

HADDEN, ANN, born 1785, wife of David Hadden, died in New
York 3.9.1845. [AJ#5100]

HAIN, ALEXANDER, born 1817, from Auchtermuchty, Fife, died in
Toronto 25.2.1900. [PJ]

HALDANE, JOHN, born in Scotland, died in New York 12.6.1849.
[EEC#21825]

HALKET, Reverend ANDREW, minister of St Andrew's, St John's, New Brunswick, married Frances Ann Taylor, eldest daughter of William Taylor in Fredericton, New Brunswick, there 12.6.1844. [W#5.482]

HALL, JANET, daughter of Alexander Hall, married Andrew Arthur a shipbuilder in New York, in Paisley 28.3.1848. [SG#1704]

HALL, JOHN, second son of Alexander Hall a wood-merchant in Fisherrow, Edinburgh, died in New York 31.1.1845. [EEC#21219]

HALL, THOMAS PARK, born 1823, second son of Captain Alexander Hall in Greenock, Renfrewshire, was drowned off St John, Newfoundland, 19.7.1848. [SG#1740]

HAMILTON, CATHERINE, late of Montreal, Canada, married Reverend Archibald Duff, in Fraserburgh, Aberdeenshire, 2.4.1841. [AJ#4891]

HAMILTON, ELIZA, youngest daughter of Captain John Hamilton in Troon late merchant in Ayr, married John Montgomery, Dalhousie, New Brunswick, in Troon, Ayrshire, 6.2.1834. [AJ#4493][SG#217]

HAMILTON, GEORGE, Hawkesbury, died in Hawkesbury, Upper Canada, 7.1.1839. [SG#742]

HAMILTON, GEORGE COLQUHOUN, of Bardownie, Canada West, married Charlotte Allardice of Murlingden, Angus, at Murlingden, Canada West, 20.3.1855. [EEC#22728]

HAMILTON, JAMES, in New Orleans, married Jane, eldest daughter of W. Duncan, a writer in Hamilton,Lanarkshire, at Wishaw, Lanarkshire, 9.10.1832. [FH#554]

HANDYSIDE, ROBERT, eldest son of David Handyside in Peffermill, died in Montreal 20.7.1844. [EEC#21073][W#5.493]

HARDY, ..., son of W.F.Hardy, born in St Louis, Missouri, 26.12.1861. [EEC#23681]

HARCUS, ALEXANDER, son of Alexander Harcus a builder in Burntisland, Fife, died in Detroit 22.8.1873. [FFP]

HARKNESS, ALEXANDER, late a teacher of the Free Middle Church School in Paisley, Renfrewshire, died in Philadelphia 6.10.1849. [SG#1870]

HARLEY, WILLIAM, born 1807, third son of William Harley, Willowbank, Glasgow, died on Campobello Island, near St Andrews, New Brunswick, 5.7.1834. [SG#275]

HARPER, ..., son of Reverend James Harper, born 12.9.1838 in Ellicott, Baltimore, USA. [SG#726]

HASLES, DAVID, and his wife Elizabeth Thom, from
Heatherstacks Farm, Forfar, Angus, later in USA 28.6.1850.
[SRO.RS.Forfar#16/117]

HAY, AGNES, in Cincinatti, youngest daughter of Reverend
William Scott Hay in Midmar, Aberdeenshire, late from
Renfrewshire, married Reverend Isaac Russell, in Chicago
19.6.1862. [AJ#5975]

HAY, JANET STEWART, born 1856, third daughter of Peter Hay a
farina manufacturer in Glen Eden House, Fife, wife of Patrick
William Stephen, died in Philadelphia 28.12.1876. [FH]

HAY, ..., daughter of Dalrymple Hay, born in Halifax, Nova
Scotia, 3.4.1859. [EEC#23356][CM#21713]

HEDGE, Mrs LOUISA, wife of Reverend Henry Wilkes, formerly of
Albany Street Chapel, Edinburgh, died in Montreal 8.9.1838.
[AJ#4737]

HEGAN, ..., son of John Hegan, born in St John's, New
Brunswick, 28.8.1844. [W#5.499]

HEITELIE, WILLIAM, born 1783, from Duncliffe, Edinburgh, died in
Dunedin Park, Mosa, Canada West, 9.2.1855. [EEC.22719]

HENDERSON, ELIZA, youngest daughter of Captain James
Henderson in Glasgow, married Robert Steel, Monklands
Mill, Fergus, at Hagsville, Toronto, 15.1.1857. [EEC#21042]

HENDERSON, ..., born in Scotland 1793, a merchant, arrived in
Boston, Charlestown District, USA, late 1821 on the
schooner Cherub, Captain Shepperd. [USNA]

HENDERSON, JAMES, son of James Henderson a factor in
Lochgelly, Fife, died at Fort Clark, Los Moras River, Texas,
4.1853. [FH:12.1.1854]

HENDERSON, P.B., from Aberdeen, married Henrietta J., eldest
daughter of Simeon Sweetlie, in Kingston, Canada West,
28.11.1850. [AJ#5370]

HENDERSON, ROBERT, a joiner from Lindores, Fife, married
Mary Emma Masterton, eldest daughter of John Masterton,
in Omaha, Nebraska, 20.6.1886. [People's Journal]

HENDRY, GEORGE, born in Keith, Banffshire, 1803, emigrated to
Canada 1834, settled in Woodstock, District Superintendent
of Common Schools for Brock, Canada West, died 10.1847.
[AJ#5211]

HENNEN, CAROLINE LOUISE, daughter of Alfred Hennen, wife
of William Mure HM Consul, died in New Orleans
15.12.1851. [FJ#995][W#1293]

HEPBURN, ELLEN MARGARET, wife of Richard FitzHerbert,
Captain of the Rifle Brigade, daughter of James Hepburn,
Tovil Place, Edinburgh, died in Halifax, Nova Scotia,
21.5.1845. [EEC#21206]

HERON, GEORGE, born 1827, Buchan Farm, fifth son of Gilbert
Heron, farmer in the Mains of Birness, Logie Buchan,
Aberdeenshire, died at the Homestead, Gloucester, Ottawa,
18.7.1876. [AJ#6709]

HERON, Mrs JANE, wife of Andrew Heron, died at Niagara
6.7.1832. [AJ#4422]

HERON, ROBERT, born 1810, a printer, died in Toronto 1834.
[AJ#4430]

HODGE, HANNAH, relict of William Beveridge in Kelty, Fife, died
in Logan City, Utah, 10.2.1882. [DJ]

HODGERT, JAMES, formerly a joiner in Glasgow, then in
Plattesmouth, Nebraska, 1874. [SRO.SC20.34.41.42]

HOGG, ALISON, youngest daughter of Reverend James Hogg in
Kelso, Roxburghshire, married Reverend Thomas Goodwillie
from Barnet, Caledonia County, Vermont, in Edinburgh
11.4.1833. [DPCA, 26.4.1833]

HOGG, ISABELLA, youngest daughter of James Hogg a farm
grieve at Wemyss Castle, Fife, married Joseph Nicoll from
Montrose, Angus, in Montreal 24.4.1860, she died at
Catarague Nursery, Kingston, America, 22.12.1878. [FFP]

HOGG, KATHERINE FORBES, eldest daughter of Major General
Adam Hogg of the Bombay Army, widow of William J.
Hickes, died in Hamilton, Canada, 28.9.1859. [CM#21861]

HOGGER, JOHN, born in Dalserf, Lanarkshire, 1758, died at his
son's house near Don River, Toronto, 9.4.1851. [W#1222]

HOLMWOOD, JEMIMA ELIZABETH, infant daughter of John
Holmwood, Findon Place, died in West Flamborough, Upper
Canada, 26.9.1843. [AJ#4999]

HOLMWOOD, JOHN S., died 25.11.1847 at Findon Place, West
Flamborough, Upper Canada. [AJ#5220]

HOLMWOOD, MARGARET OGILVY, born 1838, daughter of John
S. Holmwood, Findon Place, West Flamboro, Canada West,
married John Cramer, Barkersburgh, in Waterloo, Iowa,
27.6.1861; she died in Parkersburg, Iowa, 15.5.1862.
[AJ#5925/5971]

HOME, DAVID, second son of James Home of Linhouse,
Edinburgh, commander of a Hudson Bay Company ship,
drowned in the River Columbia 1838. [AJ#4742]

HOME, JOHN, eldest son of James Home late in Edinburgh, married Mary Perkins, daughter of Reverend W. Perkins of Brunswick, in Missouri 2.1856. [CM#20855]

HONEYMAN, BETSY, born 1834, eldest daughter of John Honeyman in Auchtermuchty, Fife, wife of Thomas S. Watson, died in Heber City, Utah, 25.5.1888. [PJ]

HOOD, JAMES, born in Scotland 1787, a farmer, arrived in New York 1821 on the ship <u>Camillas</u>, Captain Peck. [USNA]

HOOD, JANE, in Los Guilucus, daughter of James Hood in Cupar, married John Spence in Bodega, in San Francisco 21.3.1857. [FH]

HOOD, JOHN, born in Scotland 1783, a farmer, arrived in New York 1821 on the ship <u>Camillas</u>, Captain Peck. [USNA]

HOOD, PETER, born in Scotland 1793, a farmer, arrived in New York 1821 on the ship <u>Camillas</u>, Captain Peck. [USNA]

HOOD, ROBERT, second son of George Hood in Santa Rosa, California, but from Cupar and Colinsburgh, Fife, died in Santa Rosa 1893. [PJ, 8.7.1893]

HOOD, THOMAS SHEPHERD, from Cupar, Fife, married Janet Anne West, second daughter of James E. West in Kingston, Jamaica, grand-daughter of Hugh Kennedy of Battersea, Manchester, Jamaica, in San Francisco 29.10.1881. [FH]

HOPE, MARY, born 1786, wife of Andrew Weal late baron officer to the Duke of Buccleugh, died in Flamboro West, Canada West, 1848. [W#604]

HOPE, ... , daughter of Adam Hope, born at St Thomas, London District, Upper Canada, 22.8.1841. [AJ#4891]

HOPKIRK, HENRY GLASSFORD, born 1819, third son of John Glassford Hopkirk, died in Kingston, Upper Canada, 12.11.1842. [EEC#20443]

HOPKIRK, JAMES, son of James Hopkirk of Dalbeth, died in Kingston, Canada, 15.10.1859. [EEC#23437]

HORNE, DAVID, born 1853, a joiner late at Dewar Place, Edinburgh, youngest son of Thomas Horne at Bridgened of Ceres, Fife, died at 67 Varick Street, New York, 15.3.1881. [FH]

HORNE, Reverend WILLIAM, late of the United Secession Church in Carnwath, Lanarkshire, died in Yorktown, Delaware County, Indiana, 17.12.1848. [SG#1793]

HOSSACK, AGNES, daughter of John Hossack late of Duffus, Morayshire, married R.C. Geggie a schoolmaster in Quebec, in Quebec 20.10.1833. [AJ#4484]

HOSSACK, CHARLES D., from Edinburgh, married Louisa Moule, eldest daughter of Joseph Moule of the General Post Office in Edinburgh, in Sacramento City, California, 3.3.1857. [EEC#23039]

HOSTLER, DAVID, born in East Fife, lessee of the Kellie Colliery, died at his son's residence in Leeds, Canada, 6.3.1873. [FH]

HUGH, ..., daughter of Thomas Hugh from Wemyss, Fife, born at Little Sawmill Run, Alleghany County, Pennsylvania, 31.3.1870. [FA]

HUME, JAMES, born in Georgia 27.3.1747, educated in Scotland, Attorney General of Georgia, Lord Chief Justice of East Florida, a Loyalist, died in Leadervale, Earlstoun, Berwickshire, 12.4.1839. [EEC#119987]

HUME, Reverend WILLIAM, born in Urr, Dumfries-shire, 1770, educated at the University of Edinburgh, 30 years in Nashville, died in Nashville, Tennessee, 23.5.1833. [SG#156]

HUNTER, MARGARET CLAPPERTON, daughter of Reverend John Hunter, married John Johnston of the Marine and General Fire Insurance Company Bank of Milwaukee, Wisconsin, at Savock of Deer, Aberdeenshire, 12.6.1861. [AJ#5919]

HUTCHESON, AGNES, born 1839, second daughter of David Hutcheson a blacksmith in Strathmiglo, Fife, died in Jersey City, New Jersey, 2.5.1896. [PJ]

HUTCHESON, ALEXANDER FRASER, eldest son of John Hutcheson, Moyness, Nairnshire, died in Montreal 19.11.1846. [AJ#5168][EEC#211450]

HUTCHISON, ALEXANDER, born 1837, youngest son of Henry Hutchison a skinner in Cupar, Fife, married Janet Morrison, second daughter of David Morrison late Colonel of the 79th New York Volunteers, in New York 21.6.1867. [FA]; he died in New York 5.10.1871. [PJ]

HUTCHISON, JOHN, MD, born 1797, from Kirkcaldy, Fife, died in Montreal 1.8.1847. [AJ#5202][EEC#21554]

HUTCHISON, JOHN, from Cupar, Fife, died at Plum Creek, Manitoba, 10.12.1885. [PJ]

HUTCHINS, WILLIAM, born in Scotland 1800, a merchant, arrived in Savannah, USA, on the ship Georgia, Captain Varnum, late 1821. [USNA]

HUTT, EUPHEMIA, wife of Andrew Deas, daughter of Andrew Hutt in Colinsburgh, Fife, died in Brooklyn, New York, 24.7.1888. [FJ]

HUTTON, MARY, eldest daughter of David Hutton in Cupar, Fife,
wife of ... Bolion, died in Santa Rosa, California, 25.1.1854.
[FH]

HUTTON, MARY, youngest daughter of Thomas Hutton in Cupar,
Fife, married Alexander Reekie from Collernie, Fife, in
Detroit 20.3.1861. [FH]

HYNDMAN, HENRY, second son of Colonel Hyndman HEICS,
died in Goderich, Upper Canada, 19.9.1844.
[EEC#21099][W#5.510]

HYSLOP, THOMAS LOGAN, youngest son of W. Hyslop of
Blackcraig, died in New York 1.11.1851. [W#1279]

INGLIS, FRANCES ERSKINE, third daughter of William Inglis,
WS, married Chevalier Calderon de la Barca, Spanish
minister in Washington, in New York 24.9.1838. [AJ#4738]

INGLIS, JAMES, eldest son of Andrew Inglis the parochial
schoolmaster of Dalgetty, Fife, died in St Louis 2.7.1860.
[FA]

INGLIS, Mrs ..., widow of William Inglis in Edinburgh, died in
Baltimore 11.2.1848. [AJ#5228][EEC#21632]

INNES, ANNE M, eldest daughter of John Innes from Cupar, Fife,
married Jacob J. Stuart, in New York 19.10.1875. [FH]

INNES, JESSIE FRANCES, second daughter of John Innes,
married Charles William Bohlken, in New York 25.1.1876.
[FH]

INNES, JOHN, a master engineer, eldest son of Andrew Innes in
South Bridge, Cupar, Fife, died in New York 24.8.1882. [FH]

INNES, MARGERY, daughter of John Innes a merchant tailor in
Aberdeen, and wife of Alexander Hay, died in Watertown,
Jefferson County, New York, 9.6.1848. [AJ#5244]

IRELAND, ALEXANDER TAYLOR, born 1864, second son of
Thomas Ireland in Crail, Fife, died in Brooklyn, New York,
11.1.1886. [PJ]

IRVINE, DAVID M., eldest son of Robert Irvine, 18 Buccleuch
Place, Edinburgh, died in New York 23.1.1856.
[CM#207710]

IRVINE, PETER, born 1772, brother of Washington Irvine and Mrs
Van Wart in Birmingham, died in New York 1838. [AJ#4728]

IRVING, ROBERT, a stonemason in Nevada 22.8.1877.
[SRO.RS.Annan#15/163]

IRVING, WILLIAM, a farmer at Port Mary then in USA 5.7.1872.
[SRO.RS.Annan#13/281]

IRVING, WILLIAM, in Prince Edward Island 8.11.1865.
[SRO.RS.Annan#12/65]

JACK, PETER, born in Leven, Fife, 1.1826, a banker, died in
Halifax, Nova Scotia, 8.2.1888. [PJ, 25.2.1888]

JACK, ..., daughter of David Jack, born in New York 9.7.1856.
[CM#20855]

JACK, ..., son of David Jack, born in New York 19.9.1857.
[EEC#21251]

JACKSON, GEORGE, born 1811, of Jackson and Robins of New
York, "he travelled for several years for Messrs Raimes and
Company of Edinburgh", died in Brooklyn 26.11.1851.
[FJ#990]

JACKSON, or COCK, HELEN, in USA 13.8.1860.
[SRO.RS.Annan#10/276]

JACKSON, HENRY, eldest son of ..... Jackson in Musselburgh,
Midlothian, died in New York 2.2.1849.
[EEC#21825][SG#1829]

JAMIESON, GEORGE GRANT, WS, died in Toronto 14.8.1834.
[AJ#4527]

JAMIESON, WILLIAM, a farmer from Touxhill, New Deer,
Aberdeenshire, died in Oxford township, Kent County,
Canada West, 8.10.1862. [AJ#5994]

JAMIESON, ... son of William Jamieson jr., born 16.10.1862 in
Oxford township, Kent County, Canada West. [AJ#5994]

JEFFREY, ISABELLA, youngest daughter of John Jeffrey a writer
in Edinburgh, married Reverend B.C.Hill, York, Upper
Canada, at the house of John McConnel, Markbroom,
Canandaigua, New York, 8.11.1841. [AJ#4902]

JEFFREY, JOHN, late minister of the Reformed Church in
Quarrelwood, Kirkmahoe, died in New York 25.12.1831.
[AJ#4387]

JEFFREY, JOHN, from Puddledub, Dunfermline, died in Chicago
17.3.1871. [FH]

JOHNSON, RICHARD, a merchant in Montreal, married Grace,
fourth daughter of Peter McKeich in Port Glasgow, 4.4.1831
[AJ#4366]

JOHNSON, WILLIAM, Captain of the Royal Navy, son of William
Johnson of Petterlaw and Foulden, Berwickshire, died in
Georgina, Upper Canada, 28.3.1851. [FJ#959]

JOHNSTONE, Mrs ALICE, born 1786, wife of Reverend John
Johnstone late of Glasgow, died in Jersey City, New York,
26.7.1849. [SG#1847]

JOHNSTON, DAVID, born in Scotland 1768, arrived in Savannah,
USA, on the ship Georgia, Captain Varnum, late 1821.
[USNA]

JOHNSTONE, EBENEZER WILLIAM, second son of Reverend
Thomas Johnstone in Dalry, Ayrshire, died in Skeldon,
Upper Canada, 26.8.1839. [SG#809]

JOHNSTON, GEORGE, son of John Johnston, born 19.7.1862,
died 5.9.1862 in Milwaukee, Wisconsin. [AJ#5980/5987]

JOHNSTON, GILBERT, in New York 1837. [SRO.RD5.571.340]

JOHNSTON, JOHN, in Knoxville, Knox County, Illinois, and his
wife Ann Mitchell, daughter of Captain Andrew Mitchell of
the Fifeshire Militia in Cupar, Fife, 2.7.1842.
[SRO.B13.8.2.163-168]

JOHNSTON, JOHN, youngest son of Andrew Johnston a
merchant in St Monance, Fife, emigrated to Canada 1849,
settled in Chatham, Ontario, died there 10.1899.
[EFR,8.12.1899]

JOHNSTONE, MARGARET, second daughter of Alexander
Johnstone, North Broadford, Aberdeen, married Arthur
Simpson, Brant, Bruce County, Canada West, at Toronto
14.11.1861. [AJ#5940]

JOHNSTON, WILLIAM, born in Scotland 1791, with 5 children,
arrived in New York on the ship Camillas, Captain Peck,
1821. [USNA]

KAY, ALEXANDER, third son of John Kay in Hilton of Carslogie,
Fife, died in Pelham, Upper Canada, 4.3.1845. [FH]

KAY, DAVID, born in Markinch, Fife, 1807, a blacksmith, died in
New York 11.11.1851. [FH]

KEAY, PATRICK, from Glasgow, educated at King's College,
Aberdeen, graduated MA 3.1845, later a missionary in
Nashwaak, New Brunswick. [KCA#297]

KEIR, ANNIE, late from London, married Reverend Frederick
Busch, pastor of the German Reformed Church in New York,
in New York 1850. [W#XI.1097]

KEITH, JOHN, born 1813, from Foodieash, Fife, died in Fraer,
Iowa, 30.5.1894. [PJ]

KEITH, LEWIS, youngest son of Reverend William Keith in
Golspie, died in Halifax, Nova Scotia, 6.1843. [AJ#4984]

KEITH, ROBERT, born 1840, a bootmaker from Auchtermuchty,
died at his son's residence at Goldfield, Wright County, Iowa,
18.11.1892. [PJ]

KELLIE, JOHN J., from Haddington, died in Vauckieckhill, Canada
West, 12.1.1855. [EEC.22700]

KEMP, CHARLOTTE AUGUSTA, wife of Henry Kemp a merchant,
died in New York 31.12.1850. [EEC#22072]

KEMPT, ALEXANDER, born 1812, died in Petersburgh, Canada, 22.7.1876. [AJ#6709]

KENNEDY, ANNA GRACE, widow of Dr Kennedy in Leven, Fife, married James B.Mackie, Abingdon, Illinois, in Brooklyn, New York, 19.4.1881. [FFP]

KENNEDY, JOHN, Upper Canada, youngest son of David Kennedy of Knocknalling, married Jane Maxwell Carsan, eldest son of William Carsan, writer in Dumfries, at Pleasance, Dumfries, 10.4.1834. [SG#236]

KENNEDY, JOHN, in Bermuda 1838. [SRO.RD5.592.374]

KENNEDY, MARGERY MUTTER, eldest daughter of Reverend Andrew Kennedy from Leith, Banffshire, married J.C.Patullo, at Mount Juan Farm, London, Canada, 9.10.1862. [AJ#5992]

KENNY, JOANNA, daughter of Edward Kenny the President of the Legislative Council of Nova Scotia, married Bowes Daly, in Halifax, Nova Scotia, 4.7.1859. [CM#21792]

KERR, ELIZA, second daughter of William Kerr a merchant from Paisley, married Donald Mackay, a merchant, in Montreal 30.7.1833. [SG#177]

KERR, ISABELLA, daughter of David Kerr and granddaughter of Reverend David Ross in Burntisland, married Alexander McKenzie Ross, in Quebec 14.12.1854. [FJ]

KERR, J.C., in Upper Canada, 1836. [SRO.RD5.549.646]

KERR, JAMES HASTINGS, died in Quebec 30.12.1845. [AJ#5118]

KERR, JESSIE, born 1807, wife of Charles Tait, died in Montreal 2.6.1839. [SG#782]

KERR, MARIA, born 1825, wife of David Ross from Burntisland, died in Quebec 27,11,1854. [FH]

KERR, THOMAS, from Aberdeen, married Sarah Jane, youngest daughter of Thomas Jacox, in Saltspringville, Montgomery County, New York, 1.10.1845. [AJ#5105]

KERR, WILLIAM, aged 14 months, son of Thomas Kerr in Sharon, Wisconsin, late of Aberdeen, died 18.9.1847. [AJ#5207]

KETTLE, THOMAS YOUNG, eldest son of Reverend Thomas Kettle in Leuchars, Fife, died in Savanna, Georgia, 6.8.1832. [EEC#18861]

KEVAND, ALEXANDER, a schoolmaster in Wickham, Queen, New Brunswick, 17.8.1818. [SRO.RS.Wigtown#1/248]

KEY, WILLIAM INGLIS, born 1816, son of John Key {1791-1823} a brewer in Crail, Fife, a merchant in New Orleans, died at 107 Gaienne Street, New Orleans, 5.4.1868. [FH]

KIDD, JAMES, from New Deer, Aberdeenshire, educated at King's College, Aberdeen, graduated MA 3.1851, later a minister in New Brunswick. [KCA#303]

KIDD, JESSY, wife of John Kidd, fourth daughter of Thomas Denham the Assistant Clerk of Session in Edinburgh, died in Toronto 24.5.1841. [EEC#20221]

KIDD, NINIAN SELKIRK, from Burntisland, married Carrie Louise Rankin, daughter of John C. Rankine, at Mount Vernon, New York, 8.7.1890. [FFP]

KIMBALL, EBENEZER, died in New York 11.6.1888. [DJ]

KINCAID, MARGARET, daughter of Thomas Kincaid a merchant in Leith, married Alexander Rowand MD from Montreal, in Edinburgh 25.12.1843. [W#5.430]

KING, JANE, born 1833, youngest daughter of William King late of Edinburgh, died in Canandaigna, USA, 6.12.1849. [W#1071]

KING, Reverend WILLIAM, born 1790, for 24 years minister of the Church of Scotland in the Presbytry of London, Canada West, died in Carradoc, Canada West, 13.3.1859. [CM#21770]

KINGSTON, JOSEPH, born in Scotland 1781, a laborer, with Margaret born 1786, and 2 children, arrived in Barnstable, USA, late 1821 on the schooner Alert, Captain Pease. [USNA]

KINLOCH, ROBERT A.G., youngest son of Sir George Kinloch of Kinloch, died in New York 21.7.1882. [FFP]

KINNEAR, JOHN, born 1834 in Buckhaven, Fife, died in New York 17.8.1872. [PJ]

KINNEAR, MARGARET, born 1824, widow of David Anderson in Cupar, died in Leaneck, New Jersey, 28.2.1896. [PJ]

KINNEAR, THOMAS, son of Thomas Kinnear of Kinloch, Fife, died at Richmond Hill, Yonge Street, Toronto, 29.7.1843. [EEC#20653]

KINNELL, DAVID, born 1835, son of James Kinnell in Cupar and Leven, died in Montreal 8.1.1892. [PJ]

KIRK, ANN, daughter of James Kirk, relict of Robert Balfour, died in Toronto 1882. [PJ:15.7.1882]

KIRK, DAVID, engineer in West Farnham, Montreal, 1862. [SRO.SC20.34.34.134/137]

KIRK, JAMES, born 1810, from Ceres, Fife, died at Lake Crystal, Blue Earth, Minnesota, 6.2.1875. [PJ]

KIRK, WILLIAM, born in Dunfermline 1746, served in the first American war, then settled in Pictou, Nova Scotia, died in St Mary's, Antigonish, 9.8.1843. [SG#1228]

KIRKWOOD, JOHN, born in Stirling, died at Long Point, Montreal, 20.8.1832. [AJ#4422]

KNIGHT, ROBERT, Pape Castle, Cockermouth, Cumberland, died in Galt, Upper Canada, 1.8.1834. [SG#295]

KNIGHT, Dr WILLIAM, born in Aberdeen, Professor of Moral Philosophy at the University of Georgetown, died in Georgetown, Kentucky, 21.3.1837. [DPCA#1826]

KNOWLES, LUKE, born in Scotland 1788, a cooper, arrived in Boston, Charlestown District, USA, late 1821 on the sloop Katy Ann, Captain Fisher. [USNA]

LAIDLAW, ADAM, a merchant in Howard, married Mary Gillis, in London, Canada West 20.3.1845. [EEC#21191]

LAIDLAW, ADAM, son of William Laidlaw in Peebles-shire, died in Morpeth, Canada West, 13.5.1855. [EEC.22747]

LAIDLAW, ROBERT, son of William Laidlaw, Horsburgh Castle, Peebles-shire, died in Raleigh, Canada West, 25.3.1847. [EEC#21502]

LAIDLAW, WILLIAM, a merchant in Halifax, Nova Scotia, then in Ship Row, Aberdeen, died there 20.2.1833. [AJ#4442]

LAING, ..., daughter of P.S.Laing, staff assistant surgeon, born in Bytown, Canada West, 18.10.1848. [EEC#21739]

LAING, ..., son of James Laing in Berbice, born in New York 25.8.1848. [SG#1752]

LAIRD, JOHN, died in Georgetown, USA, 11.7.1833. [AJ#4468]

LAIRD, SAMUEL, born in Scotland 1801, a laborer, arrived in New York on the ship Camillas, Captain Peck, 1821. [USNA]

LAIRD, WILLIAM, son of David Laird in Glasgow, died in Mobile, USA, 13.5.1849. [SG#1827]

LAMB, JAMES, from Fordell, Fife, died at the residence of his son-in-law R.P.Stratheam, Senega, Ventura County, California, 12.11.1884. [DJ]

LAMB, JANE PATRICK, youngest daughter of David Lamb, Rossie Toll, Auchtermuchty, married John Reid, from Banff, of Flushing, Long Island, in New York 23.3.1871.[PJ]

LAMB, MARY, second daughter of James Lamb, married Robert Perkins Stratheam in Carpentaria, Santa Barbara, California, 7.11.1879. [FA]

LAMB, WILLIAM, born 1789 in Ceres, Fife, a music teacher, died at his brother-in-law's home 26, 7th Street, Fall River, Massachusetts, 30.4.1872. [EFR: 24.5.1872]

LANG, WILLIAM, from Glasgow, died in Milwaukee, Wisconsin, 16.1.1850. [W#XI.1086]

LANGAM, JULIA, wife of James Leslie a merchant in Montreal,
    died in St Mary's Cottage, Montreal, 3.8.1834. [AJ#4522]
LAUDER, WILLIAM, in North Carolina, 1827. [SRO.RD5.337.556]
LAUDER, WILLIAM, late a merchant in Edinburgh, died in
    Cobourg, Canada, 29.6.1850. [W#XI.1136]
LAURIE, MARGARET S., daughter of George Laurie in Miramachi,
    died in Cambridge, Boston, Massachusetts, 15.5.1850.
    [AJ#5348]
LAURIE, PETER, late of Urrall, Wigtonshire, died in Stamford,
    Connecticut, 13.12.1858. [CM#21614]
LAW, JOHN, youngest son of David Law in Brunton, Fife, died at
    90 Seldeen Street, Detroit, 13.4.1879.[PJ]
LAWRENCE, CHRISTINA, born 1821, wife of Dr John Lawrence in
    Galt, Upper Canada, died 26.5.1850. [AJ#5347]
LAWSON, WILLIAM, eldest son of John Lawson of Cairnmuir,
    died at Cairnmuir, Zorra, Upper Canada, 11.6.1847.
    [EEC#21526]
LAWSON, ..., son of James Lawson, born in New York 4.10.1849.
    [SG#1867]
LAYTON, SARAH EUGENIA, born 1847, eldest daughter of Dr
    Layton, died in Manitowaning, Canada West, 30.11.1858.
    [CM#21648]
LAYTON, ..., son of Dr Layton, born in Manitowaning, Canada
    West, 1.11.1858. [CM#21648]
LEACH, ..., son of Reverend W.T.Leach, born in Toronto
    13.5.1838. [SG#671]
LEAPER, JAMES, born in the parish of Glass, Aberdeenshire,
    1770, emigrated to Pictou, Nova Scotia, 1815, died in New
    Annan, Nova Scotia, 21.6.1838. [AJ#4721]
LECKIE, JOHN, eldest son of Reverend Thomas Leckie in
    Peebles, died in New York 22.8.1841. [AJ#4889]
LEE, ALLAN, born in Scotland 1776, a laborer, arrived in New
    York 1821 on the ship Camillas, Captain Peck. [USNA]
LEECH, WILLIAM, third son of John Leech minister of the
    Secession Church in Largs, died in Vernon, Mississippi,
    1831. [AJ#4384]
LEES, ..., son of G. TURBAYNE LEES, from Cupar, of the
    Canadian Bank of Commerce, born 24.12.1882 in Toronto.
    [FH]
LEITCH, ANDREW, born 1841, eldest son of David Leitch a joiner
    in South Fernie, Fife, killed at Reagan Falls, Texas,
    2.4.1876. [FH]

LEITCH, WILLIAM, born in Rothesay, Bute, 1814, graduated BA
1837, MA 1838, and DD 1860, Principal of Queen's College,
Canada, 1859-1864, died in Kingston, Canada, 9.5.1864.
[RGU]

LEITH, GEORGE WILLIAM, son of George Leith, born in
Hamilton, Upper Canada, 10.8.1840, died at Craigleith,
Hamilton, 23.8.1840. [EEC#20100/20107]

LESLIE, DAVID YOUNG, in Tulloch, Canada West, married
Margaret, second daughter of Bernard McFaul, in
Ogdenburg 16.7.1844. [AJ#5043]

LESLIE, ..., son of David Young Leslie, born in Tullich, Canada
West, 29.8.1845. [AJ#5100]

LESLIE, HELEN, wife of James Carter, died in Chicago 1861.
[AJ#5961]

LESLIE, JOHN, from Burntisland, Fife, married Eliza Knox, eldest
daughter of John Knox, in New York 8.2.1875. [FH]

LESSLIE, WILLIAM, of Lesslie Brothers in Toronto, son of Edward
Lesslie in Dundee, died in Toronto 17.4.1843. [AJ#4978]

LEYS, JOHN, born 1791 in Aberdeen, an engineer, emigrated
1826, settled in Toronto, died in St Croix, Leeward Islands,
8.4.1846. [AJ#5133]

LILLIE, SUSAN, from Scotland, married Adam Pearson, from
Scotland, in New York 6.5.1840. [EEC#20061]

LINDSAY, DAVID, a papermaker in Rothes Mill, Fife, died in
Saugreties, Ulster County, New York, 5.2.1831.
[FH:17.3.1831]

LISTER, TOM, infant son of Henry Lister a plumber from Cupar,
died in Wilkes Barre, Pennsylvania, 18.11.1873. [PJ]

LITTLEJOHN, THOMAS, a storekeeper at Market Wharf, St John,
New Brunswick, 8.1.1862. [SRO.RS.Culross#4/18]

LOCKE, CATHERINE, widow of James Bruce the naval officer at
Leith, died in St John's, New Brunswick, 4.2.1834. [AJ#4501]

LOCKHART, JOHN INNES CRAWFORD, second son of Norman
Lockhart of Tarbrax, died in California 1.12.1848. [W#1202]

LOCKHART, ROBERT, jr., a merchant in Montreal, married
Annabella Wilson, eldest daughter of William Wilson a
merchant in Glasgow, in Kilmarnock 10.3.1857.
[EEC#21047]

LOGIE, WILLIAM, born 1793, from Buckhaven, Fife, died at the
residence of James Bonthron, a farmer in Hay, Ontario,
22.2.1884. [FFP]

LONGMORE, MARY, wife of Captain John Annand, late in Banff,
died in Gooderich, Upper Canada, 29.8.1837. [AJ#4685]

LOOKUP, ALEXANDER, born in Dumfries 1786, Convenor of the
Seven Incorporations there, a Magistrate of Dumfries, Elder
of St Michael's church there, died in Columbus, Texas,
24.6.1849. [SG#1847]

LORIMER, JOHN, born in Cupar 1793, resident of New York, died
at Hilton, Tazewell County, Illinois, 19.4.1875. [FH]

LOTHIAN, JAMES, born 1868, son of Thomas Lothian a farm
grieve in Waulkmill, died in Philadelphia 18.7.1889. [FJ]

LOWE, WILLIAM BAIRD, born 1812, a teacher in Auchterderran,
Fife, settled in Brunton's Creek, Lynchburg, Virginia,
postmaster, died 5.1881. [FA, 11.6.1881]

LUMSDEN, JAMES, born 1841, second son of Walter Lumsden a
baker in Leven, Fife, died in New York, 11.10.1871. [PJ]

LUNDIE, ALEXANDER, jr., born in Arncroach, Fife, emigrated via
Leith to USA in 1850, died in New York 30.11.1869. [EFR,
21.1.1870]

LYALL, ANDREW ALEXANDER, died in Mexico 12.1.1846.
[AJ#5125]

MCALISTER, ALEXANDER, a merchant in Pictou, Nova Scotia,
married Jane Masson, second daughter of Thomas Masson
in Kingston, Canada West, there 6.8.1844. [W#5.496]

MCALLISTER, JAMES, born 1801, a laborer, arrived in New York
1821 on the ship <u>Camillas</u>, Captain Peck. [USNA]

MCALLISTER, WILLIAM, former Sergeant Major of the 79th
Cameron Highlanders, died in Hamilton, Canada West,
16.9.1849. [AJ#5312]

MACANDREW, DAVID, in Culton then in America, 4.9.1824.
[SRO.RS.Culross#1/140]

MCCAA, WILLIAM, from Whithorn, Wigtownshire, in Beaver
County, Pennsylvania, 9.6.1835. [SRO.RS.Whithorn#2/174]

MACAULAY, LOUISA BIRCHALL, youngest daughter of Chief
Justice Macaulay of Toronto, married Henry Edward
Bennett, in Toronto 26.11.1857. [EEC#21288]

MCCALLUM, Reverend JOHN, died at the Red River Colony,
Hudson Bay Territory, 3.10.1849. [AJ#5335][W#1098]

MCCLEESE, LIZZIE, wife of James Aitken from Anstruther, Fife,
died in Brooklyn, New York, 22.8.1903. [EFR]

MCCREADY, Mrs JANET, wife of Hugh McCready a gardener,
late from Maybole, Ayrshire, died in Montreal 21.7.1832.
[AJ#4422]

MCCULLOCH, DUNCAN, in Alnasou, in the district of Lochalsh
and Plockton in Wester Ross, to emigrate to America
c.1850. [SRO.HD21/53]

Scots in USA and Canada, 1825-1875

MCCUNN, DAVID, second son of Thomas McCunn, died in
Gallipolis, Ohio, 30.4.1834. [SG#254]
MCDONALD, ANNE, eldest daughter of Robert McDonald in
Glasgow, married Reverend Thomas Clark Wilson, New
Perth, in Quebec 1.10.1832. [EEC#18875]
MACDONALD, CHARLES, from Aberdeen, educated at King's
College, Aberdeen, graduated MA 3.1850, later Professor of
Mathematics in Halifax, Nova Scotia. [KCA#306]
MACDONALD, CHARLES, son of Professor Macdonald, St
Andrews, died at Lake View, Hamilton, Canada West,
7.4.1851. [FJ#959]
MCDONALD, DONALD, late of 31 Buccleugh Street, Edinburgh,
died in Cincinatti, USA, 23.7.1850. [W#XI.1141]
MCDONALD, HANNAH, born 1773, widow of Lewis Chisholm,
died in Montreal 8.7.1847. [AJ#5197]
MCDONALD, JESSIE, second daughter of James McDonald in
Aberdeen, married Peter Geddes a bank manager in
Chicago, in New York 23.5.1862. [AJ#5970]
MCDONALD, JOHN, born 1746 in Inverness-shire, 'the last
survivor of the 500 respectable Highlanders who emigrated
in 1784', died in Glengarry, Canada, 1836. [AJ#4641]
MACDONALD, ROBERT SMITH, second son of J.D.MacDonald
Lieutenant of the Royal Navy, died in Perth, Canada West,
7.12.1849. [W#XI.1072]
MCDONALD, R.C., of Castle Tioram, Prince Edward Island,
paymaster of the 30th Regiment, died in Caphalonia
17.8.1853. [FJ#1028]
MCDONALD, WILLIAM JOHN, married Catherine Balfour Reid,
second daughter of Captain James Murray Reid of the
Hudson Bay Company, at Fort Victoria, Vancouver Island
1857. [EEC#21150]
MACDONNELL, Captain ALEXANDER, late of the Glengarry
Fencibles, late of Fechem, Glengarry, Inverness-shire, died
in Ellora, Canada West, 22.1.1850. [W#XI.1113]
MCDONNELL, ALLAN, born 1791, late Sheriff of Midland District,
died in Toronto Lunatic Asylum, 21.12.1844. [AJ#5064]
MACDONELL, ELIZABETH, eldest daughter of Colonel Ranaldson
MacDonell of Glengarry, wife of R.C.Macdonald of the 30th
Regiment, died in St John's, New Brunswick, 22.12.1842.
[AJ#4959][EEC#20554]
MCDONNELL, JOHN, born in Scotland 1798, a mechanic, arrived
in Plymouth, USA, late 1821 on the schooner Albion,
Captain Hall. [USNA]

53

MACDOUGALL, GEORGE, son of Allan MacDougall of Hayfield,
died in Peterbro', Upper Canada, 1842(?). [EEC#20345]

MCDOWELL, JANE, fourth daughter of Alexander McDowell in
Woodburn, New Brunswick, married Reverend William
Beckett, Rutherglen, 3.3.1842. [AJ#4914]

MACEUSIE, Mrs, widow of John Bain MacEusie from Aronisk in
the district of Lochalsh and Plockton, Wester Ross, to
emigrate to America ca.1850. [SRO.HD21/53]

MCEWAN, EWAN, married Jane Cobban, daughter of James H.
Cobban, Customs Controller of Alloa, in Kinston, Upper
Canada, 24.6.1857. [EEC#21154]

MCFARLANE, MARGERY, youngest daughter of Robert
McFarlane a merchant in Greenock, Renfrewshire, married
Major Alexander McQueen, at the residence of Major Allan
MacFarlane in Cheraw, South Carolina, 19.6.1851.
[W#1243]

MCFARLANE, RODERICK, born 1810, late in St Kitts and in New
York, died in Tain, Ross-shire, 10.9.1835. [AJ#4577]

MCGIBBON, Colonel JOHN, born in Paisley, Renfrewshire, 1794,
emigrated to Canada 1818, died in Dundee, Lower Canada,
13.5.1848. [SG#1731]

MCGREGOR, DAVID, in Kenmore, Osgoode, married Mary
Johnstone Cumming, only daughter of William Cumming, at
Prospect Hill Mountain, Canada West, 17.2.1859.
[CM#21660]

MCGREGOR, EUPHEMIA, born 1836, daughter of Reverend John
G. MacGregor, died in St John's, New Brunswick, 18.1.1839.
[SG#756]

MCGREGOR, HUGH, born in Perthshire 1789, Customs Collector
at Dickenson's Landing, died in Kingston, Upper Canada,
16.5.1847. [AJ#5189]

MCHARDY, ARTHUR, born in Scotland 1814, emigrated with his
parents 1834, died in Rush 29.11.1845. [AJ#5115]

MCHATTIE, ANN, daughter of John McHattie a merchant in
Aberdeen, married Reverend John Tawse a missionary for
the Presbytery of Toronto, Upper Canada, 9.8.1836; she
died 22.6.1841 at Mansfield Cottage, King, Home District,
Upper Canada. [AJ#4623/4882]

MCILWRAITH, MARTHA, daughter of William McIlwraith,
Bardrochwood, Kirkcudbrightshire, married David McEwan,
Westminster, Canada West, in New York 21.6.1852.
[W#1349]

MCINTOSH, Reverend DONALD, minister of West and Middle Rivers, Pictou, Nova Scotia, married Jane, youngest daughter of Samuel Lydiard of Halifax, in Halifax, Nova Scotia, 10.4.1839. [SG#757]

MACINTOSH, ROBERTSON, a merchant, youngest son of Neil Macintosh in Rothesay, Bute, died in Montreal 31.8.1843. [SG#1229]

MCISAAC, EUPHEMIA, born 20.11.1822, daughter of Reverend Patrick McIsaac and Amelia Wright in Comrie, Perthshire, married Dr James Robertson, eldest son of Colonel Robertson of Middleton, at Hull Prairie, Ohio, 13.3.1844. [EEC#20020][F.4.264]

MCISAAC, ANN CAMPBELL, youngest daughter of Reverend Patrick McIsaac in Comrie, Perthshire, married John Robertson of Middleton, in Perrysburg, Ohio, 31.12.1846. [EEC#21463]

MACKAY, Mrs DIANA, born 1765, from Carnachy, Sutherland, died in Pickering, Canada, 14.9.1848. [SG#1760]

MACKAY, Colonel HUGH, born in Sutherlandshire 1751, Lieutenant of the Queen's American Rangers during the War of Independence, died at Suther Hall, St George's, Lairg, New Brunswick, 29.1.1848. [SG#1697]

MACKAY, JAMES, in Port William, Franklyn County, Missouri, 3.8.1854. [SRO.RS.Forfar#17/228]

MCKAY, JAMES, of Grand Rapids, Michigan, second son of John McKay from Collessie, Fife, married Jenny L. Cameron of Osceola, Pennsylvania, there 23.2.1876. [FFP]

MACKAY, JOHN, born in Rogart, Sutherland, 1791, died at West River, Pictou, Nova Scotia, 24.6.1847. [AJ#5194]

MACKAY, JOHN, born 1803, son of Donald Mackay halfpay of the 42nd Highlanders, late in Quebec, died in New Ireland, Megantic County, Quebec, 30.9.1848. [AJ#5262][SG#1765]

MACKAY, RODERICK, born at Loch Broom, Ross-shire, 1794, died in Montreal 10.1.1841. [AJ#4861]

MCKEACHY, Reverend THOMAS, a missionary of the Reformed Presbyterian Church of Scotland, died at the residence of William Hannah, Yonge Street, Toronto, 14.8.1844. [W#5.499]

MCKEACHIE, ..., daughter of Reverend T. McKeachie, born in Galt, Canada West, 9.5.1844. [W#5.477]

MCKEAN, ANDREW, of Van Standt and McKean in New York, married Margaret Isabella Arnoldie, eldest daughter of Thomas Arnoldie MD, FRCS, in Montreal 24.9.1851. [W#1266]

MCKENZIE, CHARLES KENNETH, born 1787, former ADC to the Duke of Wellington, died in the Rainbow Coffee House, New York, 6.8.1862. [AJ#5983]

MCKENZIE, DONALD, born 1778, late British Consul in Maine, died in Inverness 29.12.1845. [AJ#5116]

MCKENZIE, DUNCAN, born in Scotland 1794, a merchant, arrived in Savannah, USA, on the ship Pallas, Captain Russell, late 1821. [USNA]

MCRAE, DUNCAN, in Ardelvie, in the district of Lochalsh and Plockton in Wester Ross, to emigrate to America c.1850. [SRO.HD21/53]

MCKENZIE, ..., daughter of Hector McKenzie of the Hudson Bay Company, born in La Chine, Montreal, 25.5.1852. [W#1338]

MCKENZIE, JOHN, born in Scotland 1781, a merchant, arrived in Savannah, USA, on the ship Pallas, Captain Russell, late 1821. [USNA]

MACKENZIE, JOHN BAIN, from Aronisk in the district of Lochalsh and Plockton, Wester Ross, to emigrate to America ca.1850. [SRO.HD21/53]

MACKENZIE, JOHN BLACKWOOD, late of Montreal, died in Hamilton 9.12.1831. [AJ#4382]

MCKENZIE, Reverend JOHN C., MA, Professor of Classical Literature and Mental Philosophy in the Free Church College in Halifax, Nova Scotia, died there 12.3.1850. [W#XI.1099]

MCKENZIE, JOHN G., in Montreal 1836. [SRO.RD5.562.367]

MCKENZIE, KENNETH, in Ardelvie, in the district of Lochalsh and Plockton in Wester Ross, to emigrate to America c.1850. [SRO.HD21/53]

MCKENZIE, KENNETH JOHN, born 1799, minister of St Andrew's Church in Pictou, Nova Scotia, died there 15.11.1838. [SG#733]

MACKENZIE, JOHN BEG, from Aronisk in the district of Lochalsh and Plockton, Wester Ross, to emigrate to America ca.1850. [SRO.HD21/53]

MCKENZIE, MARGARET, born in Ardesier, Inverness-shire, 1814, wife of Alexander Ross, died in Oakville, Upper Canada, 30.3.1841. [AJ#4875]

MACKENZIE, ..., daughter of John Mackenzie, born in Charleston, South Carolina, 10.10.1851. [W#1269]

MCKENZIE, ..., daughter of William McKenzie, born 4.5.1862 in
Mitchell, Canada West. [AJ#5974]

MACKENZIE, ..., son of Alexander Mackenzie from Edinburgh,
born in Guelph, Canada West, 2.10.1859. [CM#21869]

MCKEUN, ARCHIBALD, born in Scotland 1787, a laborer, arrived
in New York on the ship <u>Camillas</u>, Captain Peck, 1821.
[USNA]

MACKID, Mrs ..., widow of John MacKid in Watten, Caithness,
died in Goderich, Upper Canada, 18.8.1850. [AJ#5359]

MCKIDD, ALEXANDER, from Thurso, Caithness, educated at
King's College, Aberdeen, graduated MA 3.1842, later a
missionary in Canada. [KCA#295]

MACKIE, ..., daughter of Reverend James Mackie, born in
Munckton, New Brunswick, 4.8.1861. [AJ#5931]

MCKILLICAN, Reverend WILLIAM, born 1776, pastor of the
Congregational Church in Breadalbane, Scotland, died in
Lochiel, Glengarry, Upper Canada, 11.1849. [SG#1883]

MACKIMEON, JOHN, from Crimminuie in the district of Lochalsh
and Plockton, Wester Ross, to emigrate to America ca.1850.
[SRO.HD21/53]

MCKINLAY, Reverend JOHN, MA, born in Falkirk,
Stirlingshire,1788, emigrated 1817, died in Pictou, Nova
Scotia, 20.10.1850. [W#XI.1167]

MACLAGAN, ..., daughter of Dr Philip MacLagan of the Royal
Canadian Rifles, born 20.3.1848 in Amherstburg, Canada
West. [EEC#21652]

MACLAGAN, ..., son of Dr Philip W. MacLagan of the Royal
Canadian Rifles, died in Amherstburg, Canada West,
4.8.1849. [AJ#5304][EEC#21855][SG#1711]

MCLAREN, CATHERINE, daughter of Duncan McLaren in Stirling,
married Archibald Kerr a merchant, in Hamilton, Upper
Canada, 6.3.1839. [SG#767]

MCLAUCHLIN, THOMAS, from Burntisland, father of a daughter
born 18.9.1883 and a son Thomas who died 23.9.1882 both
in Ansonia, Connecticut, [FFP]

MACLAY, MARY, wife of Reverend Archibald MacLay, daughter of
William Brown a seedsman in Glasgow, died in New York
20.9.1848. [SG#1765]

MCLEA, KENNETH JOHN, eldest son of Kenneth McLea,
drowned off St John, Newfoundland, 10.7.1848. [SG#1740]

MCLEAN, JOHN, a saddler in Halifax, 1827. [SRO.RD5.349.129]

MCLEAN, J.G., a merchant in Quebec, died 30.7.1832. [AJ#4422]

MCLEAN, JOHN, and his son John, miners from Ballingry, Fife, killed at Pleasant Valley, Shoefield, Emery County, Utah, 1.1.1884. [PJ, 2.2.1884]

MCLEAN, L.A., son of Captain McLean of the 93rd Highlanders, married Eliza N. Smith, daughter of Colonel Robert Smith of Edgewood, in Edgewood, Lexington, Missouri, 15.2.1849. [SG#1820]

MCLELLAN, DUNCAN, and his wife, both born in the Highlands, emigrated to Canada 1800, died at Mount Johnson 23.7.1832. [AJ#4422]

MACLELLAN, HENRY B., died in Boston, USA, 5.9.1833. [DPCA, 8.11.1833]

MACLENNAN, JOHN BAIN, from Aronisk in the district of Lochalsh and Plockton, Wester Ross, to emigrate to America ca.1850. [SRO.HD21/53]

MCLEOD, FLORA, daughter of Donald Mcleod from Schoolhill, Aberdeen, died in Toronto 12.6.1862. [AJ#5974]

MCLEOD, KATHERINE, youngest daughter of Alexander Norman McLeod late of Harris, married M. de Bourboulon the minister from France to China, in Baltimore 28.4.1851. [W#1234]

MCLEOD, ROBERT, a saddler from Ross-shire, Scotland, married Grace, second daughter of Hugh Polson a merchant in Aberdeen, in Montreal 19.5.1834. [AJ#4507]

MACNAB, MARY STEWART, youngest daughter of Sir Alan MacNab of Dundurn, married John George Daly a barrister in Montreal, in Hamilton, Canada West, 19.9.1861. [AJ#5936]

MCNAGHTON, MALCOLM M., second son of Finlay McNaghton a merchant in Glasgow, drowned in the Mississippi River near St Louis 26.4.1843. [SG#1228]

MCNAIR, ARCHIBALD, born 1794 in Achaloscan, Killean parish, Kintyre, Argyll, died at Laurel Hill, Richmond County, North Carolina, 20.9.1839. [EEC#19979]

MCNAUGHT, JESSIE, second daughter of John McNaught in Upper Canada, married Francis Maxwell the younger of Breaoch, Kirkcudbrightshire, 24.11.1834. [AJ#4534]

MCNAUGHTON, MARGARET, eldest daughter of George McNaughton late of Aberdeen, married Samuel Vial, at Hazelgrove, Illinois, 19.11.1846. [AJ#5168]

MCNIDER, Dr, born 1815, died in Montreal 14.3.1846. [AJ#5129]

MCOWEN, PETER, born in Scotland 1795, a laborer, arrived in
New York 1821 on the ship <u>Camillas</u>, Captain Peck. [USNA]

MCPHERSON, ANDREW, 40 years in service of the Hudson Bay
Company, died in Montreal 16.8.1847.
[AJ#5202][EEC#21554]

MCPHERSON, CHRISTINA, eldest daughter of ... McPherson of
Culcabock, died in Queenstown, Upper Canada, 10.1.1837.
[AJ#4652]

MACPHERSON, DONALD, late Lieutenant of the 15th Foot, died
in Napanee, Upper Canada, 19.9.1831. [AJ#4376]

MCPHERSON, HELEN, late of Culcabock, Inverness-shire,
married John McAulay of Kingstown, in Montreal
22.10.1833. [AJ#4482]

MCPHERSON, JANE, youngest daughter of Duncan McPherson,
Gairn, Scotland, married George Ford, Brantford, in Guelph,
Canada West, 29.1.1857. [EEC#21042]

MACPHERSON, LOUISA, wife of Alexander Bain formerly of
Edinburgh, died in Buffalo, USA, 8.7.1852. [W#1353]

MACPHERSON, ROBERT, second son of Alexander MacPherson
of Elzy, Caithness, died in Nashville, Tennessee. 11.8.1838.
[AJ#4745]

MCPHERSON, THOMAS, from Ross-shire, educated at King's
College, Aberdeen, graduated MA 3.1827, later a minister in
Lancaster, Canada. [KCA#283]

MCQUEEN, JESSIE MURRAY, eldest daughter of William
McQueen in Edinburgh, married Captain Richard Pattinson
of the 92nd Regiment, in Halifax, Nova Scotia, 29.6.1849.
[EEC#21834]

MCRAE, ALEXANDER, in Alnasou, in the district of Lochalsh and
Plockton in Wester Ross, to emigrate to America c.1850.
[SRO.HD21/53]

MCRAE, ALEXANDER, a carrier in Ardelvie, in the district of
Lochalsh and Plockton in Wester Ross, to emigrate to
America c.1850. [SRO.HD21/53]

MACRAE, ALEXANDER, from Aronisk in the district of Lochalsh
and Plockton, Wester Ross, to emigrate to America ca.1850.
[SRO.HD21/53]

MACRAE, ARCHIBALD, from Bendoloch in the district of Lochalsh
and Plockton, Wester Ross, to emigrate to America ca.1850.
[SRO.HD21/53]

MACRAE, CHRISTOPHER, from Aronisk in the district of Lochalsh
and Plockton, Wester Ross, to emigrate to America ca.1850.
[SRO.HD21/53]

MACRAE, DOUGALD, from Aronisk in the district of Lochalsh and
Piockton, Wester Ross, to emigrate to America ca.1850.
[SRO.HD21/53]

MACRAE, DOUGALD BAIN, from Killillan in the district of
Lochalsh and Piockton, Wester Ross, to emigrate to
America ca.1850. [SRO.HD21/53]

MCRAE, DUNCAN, in Ardelvie, in the district of Lochalsh and
Piockton in Wester Ross, to emigrate to America c.1850.
[SRO.HD21/53]

MACRAE, DUNCAN, from Aronisk in the district of Lochalsh and
Piockton, Wester Ross, to emigrate to America ca.1850.
[SRO.HD21/53]

MACRAE, DUNCAN, from Gallahy in the district of Lochalsh and
Piockton, Wester Ross, to emigrate to America ca.1850.
[SRO.HD21/53]

MACRAE, JOHN, a tailor from Aronisk in the district of Lochalsh
and Piockton, Wester Ross, to emigrate to America ca.1850.
[SRO.HD21/53]

MACRAE, JOHN BAIN, from Aronisk in the district of Lochalsh and
Piockton, Wester Ross, to emigrate to America ca.1850.
[SRO.HD21/53]

MACRAE, JOHN, from Reraig in the district of Lochalsh and
Piockton, Wester Ross, to emigrate to America ca.1850.
[SRO.HD21/53]

MACRAE, MALCOLM, from Aronisk in the district of Lochalsh and
Piockton, Wester Ross, to emigrate to America ca.1850.
[SRO.HD21/53]

MACRAE, MARIA CORNELIA, daughter of Colin MacRae,
Mavisbank, Aberdeenshire, wife of James Sewell MD, died
in Quebec 15.7.1849. [EEC#21869][SG#1847]

MACRAE, WILLIAM, from Edinburgh, died in New York
17.10.1859. [CM#21893]

MCTAVISH, ELIZABETH, eldest daughter of John George
McTavish, Chief Factor of the Hudson Bay Company,
married Reverend James Pyke the incumbent of St James,
Vandreuil, at La Chine 23.9.1847. [AJ#5206]

MCTAVISH, JOHN GEORGE, born 1787, Hudson Bay Company,
died at the Lake of Two Mountains, Canada, 21.7.1847.
[AJ#5202]

MACTAVISH, ..., son of D. MacTavish late of Inverness, born at
Ness Side, Haldimand township, Canada West, 1843.
[AJ#5016]

MCWATT, Captain DAVID, from Liverpool, Nova Scotia, married
Mary Smith McAlpine, daughter of John McAlpine in
Glasgow, there 5.2.1857. [EEC#21020]

MCWATT, ELIZABETH, born 1821, wife of John McWatt, died in
Barrie, Canada West, 14.7.1848. [SG#1746]

MCWILLIAM. JAMES, from Old Machar, Aberdeenshire, educated
at King's College, Aberdeen, graduated MA 3.1835, later a
merchant in America. [KCA#289]

MACHAR, ..., son of Reverend John Machar, born 9.7.1841 in
Kingston, Canada. [AJ#4884]

MAIN, JESSIE, second daughter of James Main in Glasgow,
married Henry A. Hart MD, in New York 22.7.1837.
[AJ#4679]

MAIN, MARGARET, eldest daughter of James Main in Glasgow,
married Le Baron Batsford MD in New Brunswick, in New
York 22.7.1837. [AJ#4679]

MAIR, THOMAS, born 1785, from Ellon, Aberdeenshire, died in
Bellefield, Elora, Canada West, 29.3.1862. [AJ#5964]

MAITLAND, AGNES, wife of John Wilson, died in Toronto
11.11.1837. [AJ#4695]

MAITLAND, CHARLES, of the 42nd Royal Highlanders, son of
Thomas Maitland of Pogbie, died at the Royal Barracks, St
George, Bermuda, 21.4.1851. [W#1218]

MAITLAND, JAMES WILLIAM, youngest son of Thomas Maitland
of Dundrennan, Senator of the College of Justice, married
Agnes Jane O'Rielly, daughter of J.A.O'Rielly, in New York
23.1.1856. [CM#20714]

MAITLAND, JANET, eldest daughter of William Maitland in Oyne,
married William Grant, Huron District, Canada West,
24.3.1849. [AJ#5281]

MAITLAND, WILLIAM, born 1754, died in Montreal 20.1.1851.
[W#1193]

MAITLAND, ..., daughter of Stuart C. Maitland of Dundrennan,
born in New York 7.7.1844. [W#5.488]

MALCOLM, ANDREW, born 1805, in Colinsburgh, Fife, eldest son
of David Malcolm, a mason, and Isabella Bousie, emigrated
to America 1838, settled at |Rosa, Missouri, died 27.5.1878.
[FJ, 20.6.1878]

MALLOCH, ELIZABETH, wife of John Todd from Anstruther, died
at 98 Bond Street, Brooklyn, 31.7.1868. [FH]

MARCH, JAMES, born in Edinburgh, settled in Boston, died in
New York 19.11.1841. [EEC#20297]

MARR, or SCOTT, ANN, in Toledo, Ohio, 6.6.1878.

[SRO.RS.Forfar#34/255]
MARR, JAMES, late of Gullies, Aberdeenshire, died at the home
of his son-in-law David Lawson, Carlton Place, Canada
West, 19.6.1847. [AJ#5197]
MARR, JOHN, a clerk in Chicago, Illinois, 6.6.1878.
[SRO.RS.Forfar#34/255]
MARR, MARGARET, daughter of James Marr a farmer in
Pittengullie, Aberdeenshire, wife of Samuel Hill a farmer,
died in Whitby, Upper Canada, 28.3.1846. [AJ#5133]
MARR, THOMAS, born 1850, youngest son of Thomas Marr in
Crossgates, Peat Inn, Fife, drowned at Scott's Barr, Siskyow
County, California, 29.4.1875. [PJ]
MARSHALL, JOSEPH, a joiner in Canada West, 29.2.1870.
[SRO.RS.South Queensferry#4/226]
MARSHALL, ROGER, in Canada, 1848. [SRO.RD5.821.147]
MARSHALL, ROBERT, born 1848, son of Alexander Marshall in
Ladybank, Fife, a draper, drowned at St Johns,
Newfoundland, 5.8.1871. [PJ]
MARTIN, ALEXANDER, a land surveyor from Cupar, Fife, died in
Brooklyn, New York, 26.12.1842. [FH]
MARTIN, ANN, born in Scotland 1772, with a child, arrived in
Barnstable, USA, late 1821 on the schooner Alert, Captain
Pease. [USNA]
MARTIN, CHARLES, a surgeon, born 1807 son of Alexander
Martin a civil engineer in Inverness-shire, son in law of Dr
Skinner in Pictou, died in Pictou, Nova Scotia, 10.9.1841.
[AJ#4894][EEC#20277]
MARTIN, DAVID, in Brooklyn, New York, son of Alexander Martin
a landsurveyor in Cupar, Fife, died in Torquay, Devon,
30.10.1847. [EEC#21574]
MARTIN, DAVID, from Aberdour, married Grace Bishop, second
daughter of John Bishop a merchant in Johnstone,
Renfrewshire, in New York 3.4.1870. [FH]
MARTIN, ELIZABETH, daughter of Alexander Martin a land
surveyor in Brooklyn, married William Bennet a book-keeper
from Edinburgh, in New York 4.6.1853, and died in Brooklyn
8.5.1856. [FH]
MARTIN, GEORGE, late tenant in Kirkmay, died in Naperville,
Illinois, 23.3.1842. [FH]
MARTIN, JANET, third daughter of James Martin of Highlaw,
Dumfriesshire, widow of James Hervey in Chicago, died in
Montreal 1857. [EEC#23023]

MARTIN, JOHN, born in Inch, Inverness-shire, 1781, died in
　　Puslinch, Canada, 12.1.1857. [EEC#21030]
MARTIN, PETER, born 1831, eldest son of John Martin in Kelty,
　　Fife, died in Algana, Iowa, 8.2.1874. [FJ]
MARTIN, ROBERT, born in Crail, Fife, 18.7.1820, son of William
　　Martin a lighthousekeeper, a tailor, emigrated to USA 1850,
　　a Baptist minister in America, died in Hillsdale, Michigan,
　　21.7.1901. [EFR, 27.7.1900, & 16.8.1901]
MARTIN, WILLIAM, born 1810, a merchant late of New York, died
　　in Edinburgh, 4.5.1844. [W#5.460]
MASON, JEMINA M., daughter of James Mason, Bank Street,
　　Edinburgh, married John MacKenzie, a merchant in
　　Charleston, South Carolina, there 6.1851. [W#1188]
MATHESON, CHRISTOPHER, in Drumboy in the district of
　　Lochalsh and Plockton in Wester Ross, to emigrate to
　　America c.1850. [SRO.HD21/53]
MATHESON, DOUGALD, from Aronisk in the district of Lochalsh
　　and Plockton, Wester Ross, to emigrate to America ca.1850.
　　[SRO.HD21/53]
MATHESON, DUGALD, from Aronisk in the district of Lochalsh
　　and Plockton, Wester Ross, to emigrate to America ca.1850.
　　[SRO.HD21/53]
MATHESON, FARQUHAR, from Aronisk in the district of Lochalsh
　　and Plockton, Wester Ross, to emigrate to America ca.1850.
　　[SRO.HD21/53]
MATHESON, JOHN, from Aronisk in the district of Lochalsh and
　　Plockton, Wester Ross, to emigrate to America ca.1850.
　　[SRO.HD21/53]
MATTHEW, AMELIA, born 1774, wife of James Cameron formerly
　　a merchant and a banker in Dunkeld, Perthshire, died in
　　New York 23.1.1840. [EEC#20040]
MATTHEW, JOHN, born 11.6.1815 in Cupar, Fife, a carpenter,
　　emigrated to USA 1860, died in Indiana 12.1895. [FH,
　　8.1.1896]
MATTHEWSON, JANE MACKENZIE, daughter of James
　　Mathewson a merchant in Moss-side, Daviot,
　　Aberdeenshire, wife of John Morrison from the Mill of Rothie,
　　Fyvie, Aberdeenshire, died in Moore Town, Canada West,
　　2.4.1862. [AJ#5964]
MATTHEWSON, JOHN, son of William G. Matthewson, born
　　1842, died in Bradford, Illinois, 24.12.1883. [FFP]

MATTHEWSON, RODERICK, born 1831, only son of Alexander
  Matthewson, a native of Lochalsh, Ross-shire, died in the
  Scotch Settlement, Reechbridge, Williamston, Beauharnois,
  Canada, 1856. [EEC#21007]
MATTHEWSON, WILLIAM G., born 1839, son of William G.
  Matthewson a tailor in East Wemyss, Fife, settled in St
  John's, New Brunswick, 1858, died there 8.1.1892. [FFP,
  15.4.1893]
MAXWELL, ALEXANDER, youngest son of Lieutenant Colonel
  Maxwell of Carruchen, died in Galt, Upper Canada,
  1.8.1834. [AJ#4525]
MAXWELL, ANDREW, born 1820, eldest son of Alexander
  Maxwell a flesher in Letham, Ladybank, died in Meadville,
  Pennsylvania, 17.5.1873. [FH]
MAXWELL, ISABELLA, born 18.8.1831 daughter of George
  Maxwell a bookbinder in Cupar, Fife, wife of Michael Brogan,
  died in San Francisco 10.11.1882. [FH]
MEIKLE, Reverend WILLIAM, from Ayr, a minister in Anstruther
  1848-1853, then in Mobile, Alabama, 1854-1863, later in
  New York and Ontario, died in Toronto 16.12.1902.
  [EFR:9.1.1903]
MEIKLEHAM, DAVID SCOTT, MD, born 1804, son of Professor
  Meikleham of Glasgow College, died in New York
  20.11.1849. [AJ#5328][EEC#21903][SG#1882]
MELDRUM, CHRISTINA, daughter of Robert Meldrum a
  shipbuilder in Burntisland, Fife, wife of Captain Samuel
  Gibson, died in Usburne, Huron County, Canada,
  28.11.1865. [FH]
MELDRUM, JAMES, born 1822 in Crail, a barge skipper in
  Montreal, died at Chateauguay Bason near Montreal
  30.4.1900. [EFR, 25.5.1900]
MELDRUM, THOMAS, from Leven, Fife, married Jeannie
  Fleming, daughter of Mitchell Fleming, in Omaha City
  24.4.1868. [FA]
MELLIS, Mrs JAMES, late of Edinburgh, died at Grove Terrace,
  Peckham Park, Philadelphia, 1840. [AJ#4856]
MELVILLE, GRACE, wife of Hugh Campbell, and eldest daughter
  of John Melville in Pitlessie, Fife, and grand-daughter of
  William Melville in Cupar, died at 23 Moray Place, Grand
  Rapids, Michigan, 14.12.1879. [PJ]
MELVILLE, JOHN, born in Scotland 1803, a gardener, arrived in
  Boston, Charlestown District, USA, late 1821 on the
  schooner <u>Cherub</u>, Captain Shepperd. [USNA]

MELVILLE, JOHN, in East Mains of Airlie, Kirriemuir, Angus, then
in Dakota 19.4.1876. [SRO.RS.Forfar#32/54]

MELVILLE, JOHN, born 1854, late of Cults Lime Works, younger
son of William Melville in Pitlessie, Fife, died at his brother's
house in Caledonia Street, Grand Rapids, Michigan,
11.7.1882. [PJ]

MELVIN, ROBERT, late merchant in Broad Street, Aberdeen, died
in Boharm, Nicol township, Upper Canada, 26.11.1835.
[AJ#4591]

MENZIES, DUNCAN, from Aberfeldy, married Maggie Whittet,
daughter of Alexander Whittet a blacksmith in
Auchtermuchty, at St Joseph, USA, 10.10.1873. [FH]

MENZIES, ROBERT, born 1781, a farmer, with Christian born in
Scotland 1786, arrived in New York on the ship Camillas,
Captain Peck. [USNA]

MERCER, ROBERT, late of Broomhill, Saline, Fife, died in La
Grange Hospital,Tennessee, 28.3.1863. [DP]

MIDDLETON, CATHERINE, from Aberdeen, eldest daughter of
James Middleton a music teacher in Meadowbank, Bon
Accord, Upper Canada, married John Davidson in
Woodburn, Bon Accord township, Upper Canada, 1.11.1838.
[AJ#4744]

MIDDLETON, JOHN, born 1823, fourth son of Mr Middleton from
Aberdeen, died in Meadowbank, Nichol township, Upper
Canada, 4.1.1841; Mrs Middleton died 6.2.1841. [AJ#4869]

MILLER, HELEN, daughter of Robert Miller late in Markinch, Fife,
died in Detroit 13.11.1852. [FH:9.12.1852]

MILLER, JAMES, of Miller, Hamilton and Company, died in York
Street, Hamilton, Upper Canada, 6.9.1847. [AJ#5204]

MILLER, Mrs JANET, born 1791, widow of Robert Miller late of
Anderston in Glasgow, died in West Galway, Fulton County,
New York, 24.4.1856. [CM#20793]

MILLER, JOHN, in New Brunswick, 13.1.1868.
[SRO.RS.Lochmaben#7/5]

MILLER, WILLIAM J., son of James Miller a glover in Edinburgh,
died in Woodside, Philadelphia, 20.9.1839. [EEC#19964]

MILLN, JOHN, from Dundee, died in Montreal 21.9.1843.
[EEC#20673]

MILLS, JOSEPH, son of John Mills a dentist in Montrose, Angus,
married Emma, daughter of George Pidgeon Kirby, at Zone
Mills, Canada West, 7.1844. [AJ#5053]

MILLS, RICHARD PEIRSON, born 1816, fifth son of Mr Mills a
dentist in Montrose, Angus, died in Toronto 5.7.1838.
[AJ#4727]

MILNE, Reverend A., born 1844, son of Andrew Milne a teacher
from Cupar, Fife, a minister of the Canadian Free Church,
died in Beansville, Canada, 8.4.1875. [FH]

MILNE, ANNE, born 1819, wife of Reverend William Donald
minister of St Andrew's Church, died in St John's, New
Brunswick, 3.3.1850. [AJ#5333]

MILNE, ANN PETERKIN, born 1837, second daughter of
Alexander Milne a merchant in Garmouth, Morayshire, died
in St Vincent, Canada West, 4.5.1861. [AJ#5918]

MILNE, GEORGE, Cincinatti, Ohio, married Helen Eliza, eldest
daughter of Hon. George Grinnell, in Greenfield,
Massachusetts, 6.9.1847. [AJ#5205]

MILNE, MARY ANNE, eldest daughter of James Milne in Dundee,
married John, eldest son of R. Irvine of Lobo, Canada West,
in Montreal 10.6.1846. [AJ#5139]

MILNE, ROBERT DUNCAN, born at Carslogie House 1844, son of
Reverend George Gordon Milne in Cupar, emigrated to USA
1868, editor of the *San Francisco City Argus*, died in San
Francisco 1906. [FH, 13.6.1906]

MILNE, WILLIAM, born in Scotland 1796, a merchant, arrived in
New York late 1821 on the ship <u>Amity</u>, Captain Maxwell.
[USNA]

MILNE, WILLIAM, from Dundee, an engineer in Kingston, married
Marian, eldest daughter of R. Irvine of Lobo, at Delaware,
Canada West, 3.11.1847. [AJ#5214]

MILROY, ROBERT, in America 1836. [SRO.RD5.559.68]

MINTY, WILLIAM, from Ellon, Aberdeenshire, but now of
Ascension parish, Louisiana, married Eliza, youngest
daughter of William Gordon in Belhelvie, at Ellon 28.7.1849.
[AJ#5299]

MIRRIELEES, ELIZABETH, infant daughter of John Douglass
Mirrielees, Cincinatti, Ohio, died in Hamilton, Upper Canada,
25.6.1848. [AJ#5247]

MITCHELL, ALEXANDER, a surgeon, eldest son of .... Mitchell in
Nether Careston, Brechin, died in America 14.8.1837.
[AJ#4684]

MITCHELL, ANNE, daughter of Captain Andrew Mitchell in Cupar,
Fife, wife of John Johnston in Illinois, 1837.
[SRO.SC20.34.20.61/63]

MITCHELL, GEORGE, born in Elgin, Morayshire, former contractor on the Caledonian Canal, the the Duke of Sutherland's factor in Sutherland, then at the Royal Engineer Depot in Bytown, died in Kingston, Canada West, 21.8.1847. [AJ#5204]

MITCHELL, HENRY BUIST HENDERSON, born 1851, youngest son of A. Mitchell a joiner in Cupar, a horse-shoer, died in Philadelphia 6.9.1886. [PJ]

MITCHELL, JAMES ALEXANDER, born 1821, only son of Lieutenant James Mitchell of the 68th Infantry, died in New Orleans 12.12.1845. [AJ#5115]

MITCHELL, ROBERT, born in Scotland 1803, a butcher, arrived in Boston, Charlestown District, USA, late 1821 on the brig Missionary Captain Sears. [USNA]

MITCHELL, WILLIAM, in Virginia, 1830. [SRO.RD5.417.499]

MITCHELL, WILLIAM, a builder from Cupar, Fife, died in Madison, Wisconsin, 9.5.1861. [FH]

MOFFAT, THOMAS, son of Thomas Moffat a tanner in Musselburgh, East Lothian, died in Glasgow, MO., USA, 21.7.1846. [EEC#21413]

MOFFAT, THOMAS, late with A & C Black booksellers and compiler of the third index to the 'Edinburgh Review', died on his passage to New York 1851. [FJ#953]

MOIR, ANDREW, youngest son of Reverend Dr Moir in Peterhead, a merchant in Quebec, died there 11.8.1832. [AJ#4420]

MONCRIEFF, ANNIE DILWORTH, born 1823, wife of James Sinclair, both from Edinburgh, died in Nashville, Tennessee, 7.12.1858. [CM#21617]

MONRO, ALEXANDER, a farmer, eldest son of James Monro a farmer in Anstruther Easter, died in York County, Pennsylvania, 1.3.1884. [PJ]

MONRO, JAMES, born 1811, son of James Monro in Pictou formerly in Inverness, died in Pictou, Nova Scotia, 14.8.1841. [AJ#4887]

MONTGOMERY, Dr GEORGE, MD, died in Quebec 3.9.1830. [AJ#4331]

MONTGOMERY, ANNIE AGNES, wife of George Greenfield, died in Brooklyn, New York, 19.2.1842. [AJ#4916]

MONTGOMERY, JOHN, Dalhousie, New Brunswick, married Eliza, youngest daughter of Captain John Hamilton, in Troon 6.2.1834. [AJ#4493]

MONTGOMERY, ANNE AGNES, wife of George Greenfield, died in Brooklyn, New York, 19.2.1842. [EEC#20338]

MONTGOMERY, WILLIAM, born 1821, from Edinburgh, died at Long Beach, New Jersey, 25.8.1843. [AJ#4994][EEC#20659]

MOORE, MARTHA, born in Scotland 1781, arrived in New York on the ship <u>Camillas</u>, Captain Peck, 1821. [USNA]

MORAN, THOMAS, born in Scotland 1791, arrived in Barnstable, USA, late 1821 on the schooner <u>Alert</u>, Captain Pease. [USNA]

MORE, GEORGE, born 1823, second son of Reverend John More in Cairneyhill, Fife, died at Fort Hamilton, New York, 1862. [DJ, 29.8.1862]

MOREHEAD, JOHN, born in Scotland 1789, a merchant, with Margaret Morehead, born in Scotland 1796, arrived in Newport, USA, on the ship <u>Belle Savage</u>, Captain Russell, late 1821. [USNA]

MORGAN, DANIEL, born 1839, a mason from Crossgates, Fife, son of .... Morgan, Castiebrae Cottage, Burntisland, Fife, died in Macon, USA, 1.7.1866. [FH]

MORGAN, HENRY, born 1798 in Saline, Fife, a merchant of firm Henry Morgan and Company, Maisonneuive, Montreal, died 12.12.1893. [FFP]

MORGAN, JOHN FERNIE, born 1832, youngest son of Thomas Morgan in Radernie, Fife, died in Valley Brook, Osage County, Kansas, 12.4.1876. [PJ]

MORISON, ISABELLA, eldest daughter of William Morison, Mount Pleasant, from Peterhead, Aberdeenshire, married Peter Duncan, at Davenport, Iowa, 16.1.1862. [AJ#5957]

MORISON, JEAN, born 1796, daughter of John Morison a farmer in Stackadale, Turriff, Aberdeenshire, wife of William Moir an engineer, died at Scotch Settlement, Michigan, 29.7.1841. [AJ#4888]

MORRISON, Mrs M., in Virginia, 1830. [SRO.RD5.414.377]

MORRISON, THOMAS, cabinetmaker in Charleston, South Carolina, son of Thomas Morrison a cabinetmaker in Anstruther, Fife, 1842. [SRO.SC20.34.23.36/39]

MORISON, WILLIAM, born 1824, third son of Captain John Morison of the <u>Pacific of Aberdeen</u> died in Quebec 4.6.1842. [AJ#4930]

MORTON, ALEXANDER, in Raubsville, USA, eldest son of Henry Morton a grocer in Kirkcaldy, 1866. [SRO.SC20.34.36.265/266][SRO.RS.Kirkcaldy#13/112]

MORTON, PETER, formerly of Hunter, Rainey and Morton in
Glasgow, died in Pittsburgh, Pennsylvania, 1.10.1837.
[SG#762]

MOTERFIELD, THOMAS, born in Scotland 1793, an engineer,
arrived in Boston, Charlestown District, USA, late 1821 on
the brig Missionary, Captain Sears. [USNA]

MOXEY, LOUIS WHITE, son of John Gray Moxey from Edinburgh,
died in Philadelphia 18.8.1841. [EEC#20268]

MOYES, DAVID, from Leven, Fife, married Emily Porter, eldest
daughter of David Porter a farmer in Denver, there
22.8.1873. [PJ]

MUNRO, MARY, daughter of James Munro late of Inverness,
married James Grant, a merchant, in Pictou, Nova Scotia,
15.9.1831. [AJ#4378]

MUNRO, MARY KATHERINE, daughter of David Munro late of
Washington City, USA, died at 27 Paterson Street, Kingston,
27.7.1851. [W#1243]

MUNRO, NEIL, from Torryburn Gardens, Fife, died in Amberley,
Ontario, 31.10.1884. [DJ]

MUNRO, ..., son of Colonel Munro, born in Quebec 6.9.1859.
[CM#21844]

MURE, JOHN, a merchant in New Orleans, married Fanny
Elizabeth Carter, in London 15.7.1856. [CM#20844]

MURE, ..., son of William Mure, HM Consul, born in New Orleans
4.4.1850. [W#XI.1109]

MURRAY, AGNES, in Ayr, Canada West, 13.6.1861.
[SRO.RS.Forfar#19/210]

MURRAY, ANDREW, partner of the firm of McMahan and Gilbert
merchants in Galveston, Texas, son of Thomas Murray
LL.D. in Edinburgh, died in Galveston 6.12.1858.
[EEC#23311][CM#21623]

MURRAY, BARBARA, born in Kingskettle, Fife, 1798, widow of
Neil Walker from Leven, Fife, died in Andover,
Massachusetts, 25.9.1883. [PJ]

MURRAY, DAVIDSON MUNRO, third son of William Murray late of
HM Civil Service, grandson of Alexander Bruce MD in
Edinburgh and Barbados, nephew of David Bruce of Kennet,
Clackmannanshire, died in Canada 1852. [FJ#1004]

MURRAY, ELIZABETH, only child of Captain Francis Murray the
barrackmaster of Edinburgh Castle, married Charles
Blackburn Jones MD, at The Elms, Weston, Canada West,
7.11.1856. [CM#20952]

MURRAY, JANE, third daughter of Benjamin Murray in Thurso, Caithness, married John Oal a distiller, in Halifax, Nova Scotia, 2.10.1846. [AJ#5156]

MURRAY, ..., son of Andrew Murray, late of Blandfield House, Edinburgh, a merchant in Galveston, Texas, born in Corpus Christi 2.1.1859. [CM#21657]

MURRAY, Reverend NICHOLAS, DD, died in Elizabethtown, New Jersey, 4.2.1861. [AJ#5904]

MURRAY, ROBERT, in Canada, 1832. [SRO.RD5.458.330]

MURRAY, THOMAS, born in Scotland 1788, a merchant, with his wife born in Scotland 1795, arrived in New York 1821 on the brig Catherine, Captain Barnard. [USNA]

MURRISON, ISABELLA, infant daughter of John and Elizabeth Murrison, died at Constance Street, New Orleans, 26.5.1850. [AJ#5356]

MYLNE, WILLIAM, late a merchant in Leith, died at Lothian Cottage, Dunnville, Upper Canada, 1.10.1845. [EEC#21264]

NEIL, JOHN, married Catherine Brady, in New York 26.10.1862. [AJ#5993]

NEILL, PETER, in South Carolina, 1836. [SRO.RD5.550.625]

NEILSON, WILLIAM, born in Scotland 1781, a merchant, with 2 children, arrived in New York on the ship Camillas, Captain Peck, 1821. [USNA]

NESS, ..., son of James Ness from Wemyss, Fife, born 2.5.1860 in Concession of the King, Canada West. [FA]

NICHOLSON, DAVID, in Indianapolis 22.4.1863. [SRO.RS.Lochmaben#6/119]

NICHOLSON, MALCOLM, of the firm of S.J.Hobson of New Orleans, died in New Orleans 11.6.1833. [AJ#4464]

NICOLL, JOSEPH, from Montrose, Angus, married Isabella Hogg from Wemyss, Fife, in Montreal 24.4.1860. [FFP]

NICOL, ROBERT, son of Robert Nicol in Pitlessie Mill, Fife, died in Beaconsfield, Upper Canada, 8.7.1839. [FH]

NICOL, ..., son of James Nicol, born in Baton Rouge, Louisiana, 24.9.1841. [AJ#4896]

NICOL, ALEXANDER, married Susan C. McKinnie, relict of John McKinnie MD, in Kingston, North Carolina, 6.5.1857. [EEC#21112]

NICOL, WILLIAM, married Elizabeth Balharry, daughter of Andrew Balharry, Strathearn, Surrey, in Brooklyn, New York, 5.11.1859. [CM#21886]

NICOLSON, MALCOLM, of the firm of S.J.Hobson & Company in New Orleans, died there 11.6.1833. [SG#164]

NIVEN, JOHN, from St Monance, Fife, died in Urbanna, Illinois, 30.12.1873. [EFR]

NIVEN, SAMUEL A., eldest son of Robert Niven in Edinburgh, died in Ontario 14.11.1876. [AJ#6728]

NIXON, SUSANNAH S., second daughter of Joseph Nixon in Edinburgh, married Andrew Murray, manager of the Bank of British North America, in St John's, Newfoundland, 1.11.1842. [EEC#20443]

NOBLE, ROBERT GRIEVE, a merchant in Halifax, Nova Scotia, married Emily, youngest daughter of the late Captain John Stairs, in Halifax 3.6.1850. [W#XI.1124]

NOBLE, Mrs ...., born 1785, relict of James Noble in Stewartsfield, Old Deer, Aberdeenshire, then in Amherstburg, died at the residence of her son in law Alexander Bartlet in Winison, Canada West, 25.7.1861. [AJ#5928]

NORMAND, WILLIAM, in New York City, son of John Normand in Bank Street, Cupar, Fife, 1873. [SRO.SC20.34.40.84/87]

NOTT, WILLIAM, born in Scotland 1756, with Frances Nott born in Scotland 1766, arrived in Barnstable, USA, late 1821 on the schooner Alert, Captain Pease. [USNA]

NOTT, WILLIAM, born in Scotland 1793, with a child, arrived in Barnstable, USA, late 1821 on the schooner Alert, Captain Pease. [USNA]

O'DWYER, MICHAEL, born in Scotland 1795, a teacher, arrived in Savannah, USA, on the ship Georgia, Captain Varnum, late 1821. [USNA]

OGG, CHARLES, from Banchory-Tiernan, educated at King's College, Aberdeen, graduated MA 3.1851, later a minister in New Brunswick. [KCA#303]

OGILVIE, ALEXANDER MILNE, son of Robert Ogilvie in Leith, died in New York 26.4.1847. [EEC#21530]

OGILVY, ..., son of Walter Ogilvy, born in Hopeton, Ohio, 10.4.1848. [EEC#21652]

OGSTON, EDWARD, born 1840, son of James Ogston in Wester Fintray, died in Washington 22.5.1862. [AJ#5980]

OLIPHANT, ALEXANDER COLVILLE, second son of Major Oliphant of Over Kinnedar, Fife, died in Austin, Texas, 7.5.1882. [FJ]

OLIPHANT, JANE, eldest daughter of William Oliphant the Customs Collector of Leith, married Richard Pechard jr. a merchant in St John's, in St John's, Newfoundland, 9.6.1834. [AJ#4517]

ORMOND, HELEN, daughter of John Ormond in Leith, died in
Verdura, Florida, 27.8.1841. [EEC#20273]

ORMOND, RUSSELL, daughter of John Ormond in Leith, wife of
Joseph Chaires in Tallahassee, died in Verdura, Florida,
29.8.1841. [EEC#20273]

ORR, JOHN, a railway plate layer, son of Joseph Orr in
Sinclairtown, Kirkcaldy, lately in Burntisland, died in Montreal
15.8.1853. [FA:17.9.1853]

ORROCK, ROBERT, born 1800, a farmer from Barbarafield, Fife,
died in Vespra, Ontario, 19.4.1875. [FH]

OSWALD, JOHN, from Edinburgh, died in West Troy, Albany
County, New York, 15.11.1845. [EEC#21286]

OWLER, CHARLES B., born in Cupar, Fife, 1826, son of William
Owler postmaster, died in Boston, Massachusetts,
3.12.1890. [FH.31.12.1890]

PAGE, HENRY, in Kirkcaldy, Fife, then in New York, 6.10.1858.
[SRO.RS.Kirkcaldy#11/62]

PANTON, JAMES, late a banker in Cupar, Fife, died in Toronto
28.7.1854. [FH]

PARK, CHARLES, from Inverness, died in Hamilton, Canada
West, 6.3.1859. [CM#21497]

PARK, JOHN, born in Scotland 1761, a laborer, with Letitia born in
Scotland 1776, and 6 children, arrived in New York on the
ship Camillas, Captain Peck, 1821. [USNA]

PARKER, ALEXANDER DAVIDSON, manager of the Colonial Life
Assurance Company of Canada, married Grace, eldest
daughter of John Gibson WS, in Montreal 14.7.1848.
[EEC#21691]

PARKER, EMILY TRAILL, born 1839, eldest daughter of George
Parker of Fairlie, Ayrshire, died in Hamilton, Canada,
14.3.1857. [EEC#21078]

PATERSON, ADAM, born 1814, late of Albany Street, Edinburgh,
died in Paris, Upper Canada, 21.3.1841. [EEC#20196]

PATERSON, ADAM, late of Minto Street, Edinburgh, married
Jessie Ogilvie, daughter of David Ogilvie a merchant in
Toronto, in Toronto 6.8.1844. [EEC#21082]
[AJ#5045][W#5.498]

PATERSON, ALEXANDER, born 1806, from Springfield, Fife, died
in Esqueming, Halton County, Ontario, 14.4.1890.[PJ]

PATERSON, ARCHIBALD, second son of John Paterson of
Merryflats, died in Toronto 1.3.1850. [W#XI.1098]

PATERSON, EDWARD JAMES, born 1824, Captain of the Royal
Artillery, son of Lieutenant General Paterson, died in
Quebec 18.2.1862. [EEC#23691]

PATERSON, HENRY, born in St Andrews 1807, married Helen
McIntosh in Perth 13.11.1837, a bookseller in
Auchtermuchty, died in Schnectady, New York, 28.2.1870.
[FH]

PATERSON, JAMES, son of Reverend Paterson in Midmar,
Aberdeenshire, and his wife died in Port Dover, Upper
Canada, 15.8.1849. [AJ#5307]

PATERSON, JAMES, eldest son of Andrew Paterson from
Lassodie Colliery, Fife, died at McKeesport, North America,
23.9.1872. [DJ]

PATERSON, LILLIAS, wife of J.B.Laurie in Boston,
Massachusetts, died at 26 Findlay Street, Glasgow,
19.10.1849. [SG#1866]

PATTERSON, T.H., born in Scotland 1791, an officer, arrived in
Boston, Charlestown District, USA, on the ship Jasper,
Captain Crocker late 1821. [USNA]

PATERSON, ..., son of Adam Paterson, born in Paris, Upper
Canada, 30.8.1839. [EEC#19963]

PATON, WILLIAM, born in Lanarkshire 1779, died in Detroit
17.8.1849, his wife Christine born in Lanarkshire 1783, died
in Detroit 7.8.1849, Samuel Paton born 1826, died 7.8.1849,
George Paton born 1810, died 8.8.1849, Jane Paton born
1823, died 9.8.1849, and Mrs Eliza Baldry born 1827, died
9.8.1849. [SG#1861]

PATRICK, ROBERT, born 1792, from Buckhaven, Fife, died in
Massachusetts 14.5.1884. [FFP]

PATTISON, GRANVILLE SHARP, FRCS London, Professor of
Anatomy at the University of New York, youngest son of
John Pattison in Kelvin Grove, died in New York 12.11.1851.
[FJ#989]

PATTISON, ..., son of Godfrey Pattison, born in New York
8.10.1844. [W#5.517]

PATTON, HENRY, third son of Captain William Patton,
Devonshaw, Peebles, died in Benares, Toronto, 19.5.1855.
[EEC#22753]

PAUL, JAMES, of Invercarnie, JP, Captain of the Wisconsin
Volunteers, married Angeline, daughter of Samuel Adams,
late of New York, at Pitch Grove, USA, 21.6.1849. [AJ#5300]

PAUL, JOHN ERSKINE, second son of Robert Paul, a banker in
Edinburgh, died on passage from New York 30.1.1850.
[W#1083]

PAUL, Reverend J.T., born in Cupar 1810, died in Bolsover,
Ontario, 8.3.1884. [FH]

PEARSON, ADAM, from Scotland, married Susan Lillie, from
Scotland, in New York 6.5.1840. [EEC#20061]

PEAT, ..., born in Scotland 1799, a merchant, arrived in Boston,
Charlestown District, USA, late 1821 on the schooner
Cherub, Captain Shepperd. [USNA]

PEATTIE, JOHN, born 1.1.1830 at Balcreavie Castle, Fife, son of
William Peattie of Craigiewells, a gardener, emigrated to
America 15.11.1851, settled in Long Island and New Jersey,
died 6.2.1895. [FH,6.3.1895]

PERRY, JAMES CHALMERS, born 1797, a surgeon, eldest son of
James Perry, surgeon in Bilbo Park, Aberdeenshire, died in
Jerseyville, Illinois, 18.5.1859. [CM#21750]

PETERKIN, JAMES, born 1799, from Aberdeen and Woodside,
died in Toronto 18.3.1876. [AJ#6691]

PETERKIN, ..., daughter of William T. Peterkin of the Royal
Canadian Bank, born in Toronto 4.4.1876. [AJ#6694]

PETERS, CHARLES JEFFREY, born 1772, HM Attorney General,
Member of the Executive and Legislative Councils of New
Brunswick, died in Fredericton 3.2.1848. [EEC#21625]

PETERS, JAMES, jr., barrister at law in St Johns, eldest son of
Charles Jeffrey Peters HM Attorney General of New
Brunswick, died at the home of Robert Bell in Fountainbridge
3.7.1847. [EEC#21522]

PEATTIE, JOHN, born in Ceres, Fife, 18.6.1842, soldier of the
83rd Regiment in New York 1864-, died in New York 3.1896.
[PJ: 4.4.1896]

PHILP, JOHN, a farmer from Cupar, Fife, died at Section 24,
Montrose, Lee County, Iowa, 20.6.1884. [FH]

PHILP, THOMAS, born 1861, son of John Philp, died in Montrose,
Lee County, Iowa, 14.2.1878. [FH]

PHILIPS, MARGARET, from Aberdeen, married James
Sievewright, at Stonington, Connecticut, 22.9.1847.
[AJ#5205]

PHILIP, MARGARET MENZIES, eldest daughter of William Philip
late of Aberdeen, died in New Aberdeen, Canada West,
30.7.1849. [AJ#5303]

PITCAIRN, JOSEPH, of the house of Pitcairn, Brodie and
Company in Hamburgh, died in New York 18.6.1844.
[EEC#21059]

PLAYFAIR, JOHN SPIERS, merchant in Toronto, married
Georgina, daughter of N. Hall in Montreal, there 9.9.1852.
[FJ#1033][W#1370]

POLLOCK, DAVID, born in Scotland 1788, a physician, arrived in
Boston, Charlestown District, USA, on the sloop Katy Ann,
Captain Fisher, late 1821. [USNA]

POLLOCK, MARGARET AITCHISON, daughter of Reverend John
Pollock in Govan, married Reverend Horatio Potter, rector of
St Peter's in Albany, at Trinity Church, New York, 26.9.1849.
[EEC#21878][SG#1867]

PONTON, GRACE, in Canada, 1832. [SRO.RD5.468.749]

PONTON, Dr MUNGO, from Edinburgh, died in Woodland,
Belleville, Canada West, 16.3.1849. [AJ#5290]

POPPLEWELL, JOHN, late a manufacturer in Aberdeen, died in
New York 16.9.1845. [AJ#5103]

POTTER, MARGARET, daughter of Captain George Potter in
Greenock, married John Ellis of Prince Edward Island, in
Liverpool 4.10.1848. [SG#1757]

POTTS, ANDREW, formerly a book-keeper in Edinburgh, then
with the American Fur Company, died at Fort Mackenzie,
Upper Missouri, 25.2.1842. [EEC#20517]

PRATT, ALEXANDER, from Aberdeen, died in Bothwell, Canada
West, 6.7.1876. [AJ#6708]

PRATT, SAMUEL, from Edinburgh then in Chicago, married
Maggie Macnaspie, in New York 10.4.1856. [CM#20774]

PRINGLE, ALEXANDER, born 1777, died in Kingston, Canada,
17.9.1850. [W#XI.1157]

PRINGLE, Reverend FRANCIS, born in Fife 1747, died in New
York 2.11.1833. [AJ#4490]

PRINGLE, ..., born in Scotland 1785, a merchant, with his wife
born in Scotland 1794, and 2 children, arrived in Boston,
Charlestown District, USA, late 1821 on the schooner
Albion, Captain Ward. [USNA]

PROUDFOOT, Reverend WILLIAM, died in London, Canada
West, 16.1.1851. [W#1195]

PURVES, BURRIDGE, second son of Burridge Purves of
Glassmount, Fife, died at his plantation on the Yazoo, North
America, 1.9.1837. [DPCA#1839]

PURVES, JOHN HOME, second son of Sir Alexander Purves of
Purves Hall, HM Consul, died in Pensacola 30.9.1827.
[EEC#18146]

PURVES, JOHN, eldest son of Beveridge Purves of Glassmount,
died at Oakland Plantation, near Vicksburg, Mississippi,
19.10.1850. [FJ]

PURVES, WILLIAM, youngest son of Beveridge Purves of
Glassmount, died at Oakland Plantation, near Vicksburg,
Mississippi, 23.1.1842. [FJ:10.3.1842]

PURVES, ..., daughter of William Purves, born in Charleston,
South Carolina, 8.12.1838. [SG#734]

PURVES, ..., daughter of Robert Purves, born in Springhill,
Mobile, 4.11.1840. [EEC#20145]

PYOTT, ARCHIBALD, third son of James Pyott of the Leith
Ropery Company, died in Philadelphia 22.8.1845.
[EEC#21243][W#607]

RAE, JANE, from East Calder, Midlothian, wife of George
Pearson, daughter in law of David Pearson in Arncroach,
Fife, died in Briceville, Grundy County, Illinois, 5.10.1885.
[PJ]

RAE, WILLIAM GLEN, born 1812, son of John Rae in Wyre,
Orkney, died in San Francisco 1848. [W#619]

RAE, WILLIAM, youngest son of James McGill Rae in Newbattle,
Midlothian, died in Harvey Settlement, New Brunswick,
7.6.1859. [EEC#23383][CM#21767]

RAIT, DAVID, born 1772, died in St Andrews, New Brunswick,
8.5.1838. [SG#671]

RAMSAY, HEW, from Edinburgh, married Agnes Hunter Armour,
only daughter of Robert Armour, in Montreal 6.9.1842.
[EEC#20515]

RAMSAY, JAMES, son of Andrew Ramsay in Burntisland, Fife,
married Sarah Shelton, second daughter of John Shelton, at
Paxton, Illinois, 19.2.1880. [FH]

RAMSAY, JAMES, infant son of John Ramsay from Cowdenbeath,
died in Carthage, Socorro County, New Mexico, 19.7.1884.
[DJ]

RAMSAY, JAMES, eldest son of Richard Ramsay from Cupar,
died in Fowlersville, New York, 19.12.1863. [FA]

RAMSAY, RITCHIE, born 1825, brother of David Ramsay a
clothier in Bonnygate, Cupar, settled in USA, married Helen,
daughter of Robert Russell in Cupar Mill, died in Batavia,
New York, 28.10.1908. [FH, 11.11.1908]

RAMSAY, ..., died in Montreal 13.8.1847. [EEC#211556]

RAMSAY, ..., daughter of A.G.Ramsay, born in Sandyford Place, Hamilton, Canada West, 18.9.1859. [CM#21850]

RANKEN, OCTAVIA GIBSON, infant daughter of Alexander Ranken, died in New York 29.8.1851. [W#1258]

RANKIN, AGNES, eldest daughter of James Rankin of Greenbank, Charleston County, St John, New Brunswick, niece of Hon. Alexander Rankin of Miramachi, married Captain Webster of the Royal Regiment, only son of Dr Webster in Montrose, at Greenbank 30.6.1849. [AJ#5296]

RANKIN, WILLIAM, born in Aberdeenshire, a schoolmaster, died in Middleton, Galt, Upper Canada, 6.12.1846. [AJ#5172]

RAPHAEL, JAMES, died in Philadelphia 10.3.1844. [SG#1285]

RATTRAY, ROBERT, a hatmaker late of Glasgow, seventh son of James Rattray in Coupar Angus, died in Cincinatti, Ohio, 14.2.1849. [SG#1809]

READHEAD, CHARLES EBENEZER, married Eliza Rogers, second daughter of John Rogers, in Toronto 28.9.1848. [SG#1756]

REDMOND, CHRISTIAN FISHER, born 1841, only child of Thomas Redmond in Philadelphia, died in Glasgow 23.3.1844. [W#5.447]

REED, JAMES, eldest son of James Reed MD in Kilmarnock, died in New Orleans 18.9.1839. [SG#821]

REEKIE, ALEXANDER, from Collairnie, Fife, married Mary Hutton, youngest daughter of Thomas Hutton in Cupar, Fife, in Detroit 20.3.1861. [FA]

REID, JAMES, born 1769, late Chief Justice of the Court of Queen's Bench, died in Montreal 19.1.1848. [AJ#5224]

REID, JAMES, youngest son of ..... Reid a farmer in Parbroath, Fife, died in Springfield, Mobile, 25.9.1843. [FH]

REID, JOHN HOPE, third son of .... Reid a farmer in Parbroath, Fife, a merchant in Savanna, Georgia, died in New York 16.9.1848. [FH]

REID, WILLIAM, from Kildrummy, Aberdeenshire, educated at King's College, Aberdeen, graduated MA 3.1833, later a minister in Toronto. [KCA#288]

REID, Reverend WILLIAM, Grafton, married Harriet, daughter of William Street, Countess Weir, Devon, in Cobourg, Canada West, 9.2.1848. [AJ#5232]

REITH, MARGARET, wife of James Burness late a farmer in the Mains of Barras, died in Kinnaird, Canada West, 15.9.1847. [AJ#5209]

RENNIE, JANE, eldest daughter of Richard Rennie in Glasgow, Captain of the Fife Regiment of Artillery, married Reverend D.E.Montgomery MA, of the Free Church at South Gower, Canada West, on the John Bell in Montreal 3.8.1859. [EEC#23407]

RINTOUL, AGNES, third daughter of John Rintoul of Montrose Academy, married Reverend Milo Templeton, from Troy, Miami County, Ohio, in Alleghany City, Pennsylvania, 3.8.1846. [AJ#5747]

RITCHIE, JOHN, born in Dunshalt 1818, a patternmaker in Cincinatti, died in East Walnut Hills, Ohio, 23.1.1871. [FJ, 18.2.1871]

RITCHIE, MARY, daughter of William Ritchie, Haddington Place, Edinburgh, married Thomas Davidson, at Cote St Antoine, Lower Canada, 12.9.1851. [W#1259]

RITCHIE, ROBERT, born in Dairsie, Fife, 1785, died in Ottawa 2.4.1872. [FA, 15.6.1872]

RITCHIE, SAMUEL FREDERICK, born 1844, son of Samuel Ritchie of the 78th Highlanders, grandson of R. Barclay Allardyce of Ury, died in Brooklyn, New York, 14.4.1862. [AJ#5964]

RITCHIE, ..., daughter of Samuel Ritchie, born in Hamilton, Canada, 19.5.1841. [AJ#4876]

ROBB, ANNIE, daughter of William Robb a builder in Aberdeen, married George W. Moss a merchant in Montreal, there 3.1861. [AJ#5911]

ROBB, JOHN, born in Banffshire 1793, died in Halifax, Nova Scotia, 19.3.1842. [AJ#4921]

ROBB, THOMAS, born 1816, son of Alexander Robb in Dairsie Muir, Fife, died in Leroy County, Genesee, New York, 16.12.1878. [PJ]

ROBB, ..., son of James Robb MD, Professor of Natural History, born at King's College, New Brunswick, 16.5.1844. [W#5.471]

ROBERTSON, A.R., surgeon, married Euphemia, eldest daughter of Joseph Eberts, in Chatham, Upper Canada, 3.1839. [EEC#1999898]

ROBERTSON, ALEXANDER, born in Aberdeen 1764, an artist and Secretary of the American Academy of Fine Arts, died in New York 27.5.1841. [AJ#4877]

ROBERTSON, ALEXANDER, late a farmer in Craigairn, Kemnay, died at Long Point, Montreal, 14.5.1847. [AJ#5192]

ROBERTSON, ALEXANDER, from Ladybank, Fife, married Agnes Brown, second daughter of Robert Brown miller at Arnot Mill, Leslie, at Dixon Lee, Illinois, 25.2.1868. [FA]

ROBERTSON, ARCHIBALD, born in Aberdeen 1764, a portrait painter, 44 years in New York, died in New York 6.12.1835. [AJ#4593]

ROBERTSON, CHRISTINA, second daughter of William Robertson a merchant in Dalkeith, Midlothian, married Andrew Aitchison of Jackson, Louisiana, in New Orleans 27.11.1833. [AJ#4493]

ROBERTSON, DONALD, a fur merchant, died in Montreal 25.4.1833. [AJ#4469]

ROBERTSON, ELIZA, daughter of William Robertson in Cuttlebrae, Enzie, wife of John Sutherland a merchant in New York, son of William Sutherland a fisheries officer in Cullen, died in New York 16.1.1861. [AJ#5901]

ROBERTSON, ISAAC, born 1780, late a farmer in the parish of Cairney, Aberdeenshire, died in Montreal 18.10.1837. [AJ#4696]

ROBERTSON, JAMES, in New York 20.11.1826. [SRO.RS.Dysart#2/112]

ROBERTSON, JAMES, a farmer in Still Water Village, Easter County of Washington, 1830. [SRO.GD16.35.48]

ROBERTSON, Dr JAMES, eldest son of Colonel Robertson of Middleton, married Euphemia McIsaac, eldest daughter of Reverend Patrick McIsaac in Comrie, Perthshire, at Hull Prairie, Ohio, 13.3.1844. [EEC#20020][W#5.453]

ROBERTSON, JAMES, from Balgarvie, Fife, died at Hull Prairie, Ohio, 10.8.1845. [FH:28.10.1845]

ROBERTSON, JOHN, a baker in Edinburgh later in USA, 29.9.1832. [SRO.RS.Fortrose#1/103]

ROBERTSON, JOHN, in Philadelphia, 1832. [SRO.RD5.467.126]

ROBERTSON, JOHN ALEXANDER, son of Robert Robertson a jeweller in Cupar, a dentist in Baltimore 1857. [FH: 2.4.1857]

ROBERTSON, JOHN, from Toronto, married Margaret, daughter of Hector Sinclair, Kerroward, at Petty 25.3.1841. [AJ#4866]

ROBERTSON, JOHN, of Middleton, married Anne Campbell McIsaac, youngest daughter of Reverend Patrick McIsaac in Comrie, Perthshire, in Perrysburg, Ohio, 31.12.1846. [EEC#21463]

ROBERTSON, Reverend JOHN, youngest son of John Robertson of Foveran, Aberdeenshire, died in St Paul, Minnesota, 1861. [AJ#5925]

ROBERTSON, JOHN, born 1880, son of Robert Robertson a
  miner from Hill of Beath, died in Snoe Shoe, Center County,
  Pennsylvania, 14.1.1884. [DJ]

ROBERTSON, LAURA, A., from Cupar, Fife, married Peter
  McCombie, in New York 6.10.1869. [FJ]

ROBERTSON, MARGARET, born 1788, relict of George Marr a
  shipbuilder in Anstruther, Fife, died in St Martin's near St
  John's, New Brunswick, 10.11.1876. [EFR]

ROBERTSON, PATRICK, fifth son of James Saunders Robertson,
  WS, drowned on his passage from New Orleans to Santiago
  11.9.1858. [CM#21708]

ROBERTSON, Reverend WILLIAM, born 1798, from Haddington,
  a missionary of the Seccession Church of Scotland, died in
  Canada 22.9.1832. [FH#560]

ROBERTSON, WILLIAM FORBES, born 1828, youngest son of
  Reverend William Forbes, Rosehall, Sutherland, died in
  Montreal 8.7.1849. [AJ#5301]

ROBERTSON, WILLIAM, born 1833, son of William Robertson a
  baker in Dysart, Fife, died in Miramachi 21.8.1851. [FA]

ROBERTSON, Captain, of Kinlochmoidart, married Matilda Helen
  Crawley, eldest daughter of Frederic S.Crawley, Sydney,
  Cape Breton, at Kinlochmoidart 14.5.1857. [EEC#21007]

ROBINSON, DOUGLAS, youngest son ofWilliam Rose Robinson,
  Clermiston, East Lothian, married Fanny Monroe, eldest
  daughter of James Monroe of Fanwood, New York, in New
  York 14.11.1850. [W#XI.1174]

ROBINSON, ELIZABETH, wife of Alexander Gordon late a
  Captain of the Rifle Brigade, died in Niagara, Upper Canada,
  28.7.1849. [AJ#5304]

ROBINSON, WILLIAM HENRY BUCKLE, only son of Lieutenant
  Colonel Robinson late of the 72nd Highlanders, died in
  Hamilton, Bermuda, 1856. [EEC#20989]

RODGER, D., of Montreal High School, late of Edinburgh, married
  Mary MacFarlane, eldest daughter of James MacFarlane of
  Williamston, in Packenham 16.7.1850. [W#XI.1142]

RODGER, JOHN, born 1850 in Carnbee, Fife, third son of Henry
  Rodger in Upper Kenley, killed at Whellar Store, America,
  29.1.1870. [PJ]

RODGERS, MARGARET, daughter of William Rodgers, 12
  Leopold Street, Edinburgh, married Valentine Nelson,
  St John's, New Brunswick, in Edinburgh 12.4.1838.
  [AJ#4710]

ROGER, JOHN MORICE, from Aberdeen, educated at King's
College, Aberdeen, graduated MA 3.1827, later a minister in
Peterborough, Canada. [KCA#283]

ROLLO, GEORGE, born in West Wemyss, Fife, 1857, emigrated
to USA ca.1882, killed in a mining accident in British
Columbia . [FFP, 16.3.1907]

ROLLO, MARGARET, wife of George Lumsden in Cupar, died in
Norwich, Connecticut, 10.7.1886. [PJ]

ROMANES, ROBERT ROSE, second son of Reverend George
Romanes, Professor of Moral Philosophy at Queen's
College, Kingston, died in Kingston, Canada West, 9.3.1849.
[AJ#5283][EEC#21792][SG#1807]

RONALDSON, JAMES, born in Edinburgh 1768, died in
Philadelphia 29.3.1841. [AJ#4870][EEC#20203]

RONALDSON, JOHN, in Philadelphia 1836. [SRO.RD5.547.358]

RONALDSON, JOHN, second son of Archibald Ronaldson in
Leith, died in Philadelphia 2.1.1842. [EEC#20323]

RONALDSON, WILLIAM, eldest son of Archibald Ronaldson in
Leith, his wife Helen aged 29, and their children Ellen 6,
Archibald Weatherly 4, Jane Marion 2, and Robert aged 7
weeks, died when the boiler of the <u>Lady of the Lake</u>, a steam
packet, burst near Quebec 7.9.1834. [AJ#4429]

RONALDSON, WILLIAM, born 1792, once a baker in High Street,
Edinburgh, then a farmer in Ohio, died in Chilicothe, Ohio,
3.9.1843. [EEC#20673]

ROSE, ANNE, second daughter of Edward Clouston in
Stromness, Orkney, married Augustus E. Pelly, at York
Factory, Hudson Bay, 28.8.1849. [AJ#5314]

ROSE, JAMES H., Markham, Upper Canada, second son of
William B. Rose of Rhinie, Ross-shire, died 28.3.1840.
[EEC#20063]

ROSS, CHARLES S., Assistant Receiver General, died in Toronto
15.7.1876. [AJ#6706]

ROSS, ELIZA, born in Kirkhill, Inverness-shire, 1808, wife of John
Ross of the Necropolis, died in Toronto 19.12.1852.
[W#1293]

ROSS, GEORGE, from Assynt, Sutherland, married Mary
Sutherland in Louisburg 3.9.1838. [AJ#4731]

ROSS, GEORGE CLARKE, of Culgruff, Kirkcudbrightshire, born
1798, died in Sherbrooke, Upper Canada,
1.11.1852.[W#1386]

ROSS, JEAN, eldest daughter of Donald Ross the Chief Factor of the Hudson Bay Company, married Reverend James Hunter of Cumberland Station, at Norway House, Hudson Bay, 10.7.1848. [SG#1766]

ROSS, THOMAS, MA, born 1805, Rector of Kingstown Grammar School in Upper Canada, son of George Ross the Collector of Customs in Ullapool, emigrated to Canada 1831, died 17.11.1833. [AJ#4489]

ROSS, WALTER, in Pictou, late of Tain, Ross-shire, married Elizabeth, daughter of H. Thorp in Fredericksburgh, at the residence of William Anderson in Fredericksburgh 1.12.1845. [AJ#5115]

ROUTLEDGE, JAMES, youngest son of William Routledge a manufacturer in Aberdeen, died in Brantford, Canada West, 4.3.1876. [AJ#6689]

ROW, ANN, daughter of Thomas Row a merchant in Aberdeen, married George Laing, Winchester, Upper Canada, in Montreal 14.11.1836. [AJ#4637]

ROWAND, ALEXANDER, MD, in Montreal, married Margaret Kincaid, daughter of Thomas Kincaid a merchant in Leith, in Edinburgh 25.12.1843. [W#5.430]

ROWAND, JANET, eldest daughter of Robert Rowand a farmer in Barskiven, Paisley, married Robert Wilson, farmer in Chiniacousy, Canada West, at the First Concession, Canada West, 16.5.1851. [W#1237]

ROXBURGH, ALEXANDER, born 1773, late Captain of the Glengarry Light Infantry, died in Hamilton, Canada West, 19.9.1856. [CM#20918]

ROY, GEORGE, born in Banffshire 1751, an early settler of Halifax, Nova Scotia, late a JP for Halifax County, died in Merigomish 2.7.1831. [AJ#4365][EEC#18697]

ROY, ISABELLA MAITLAND, infant daughter of Robert M. Roy, died in Niagara, Upper Canada, 16.8.1838. [AJ#4735]

ROY, JAMES, of Neathorn, died in Philadelphia 1.7.1836. [AJ#4622]

ROY, MAY WEDDERBURN, youngest daughter of Robert Maitland Roy of Belleville, married Edmund Phillips Hannaford, in Belleville, Upper Canada, 27.9.1859. [CM#21870]

ROY, ..., daughter of Robert Maitland Roy, born in Niagara, Upper Canada, 26.2.1839. [EEC#19984]

ROY, ..., son of Robert Maitland Roy, born at Bond Head Harbour, Upper Canada, 1.6.1842. [EEC#20386]

RUSSELL, ALEXANDER, sr., born 1760, died in Megantic,
  Canada East, 18.12.1847. [SG#1679]
RUSSELL, ANNABELLA, eldest daughter of Reverend James
  Russell in Gairloch, Ross-shire, wife of Roderick Matheson,
  died in Perth, Upper Canada, 10.11.1854. [EEC.22688]
RUSSELL, DAVID LAURIE, in Basaltie Canyon, Gold Gulch,
  Yuma, Arizona, son of John Russell of Middlefield, Cupar,
  Fife, 1876. [SRO.SC20.34.52.268/272]
RUSSELL, J.C., from Cupar, Fife, emigrated to America 5.1893.
  [FH: 17.5.1893]
RUSSELL, JOHN, in Philadelphia, 1827. [SRO.RD5.342.477]
RUTHERFORD, THOMAS, in America 1849. [SRO.RD5.827.289]
SALMOND, D.M.L., born 1851, MA, BA, from Aberdeen, died in
  Hamilton, Canada, 17.1.1876. [AJ#6683]
SALMOND, Mrs, wife of Archibald Salmond a currier from Cupar,
  died in Albany, New York, 17.12.1880. [FH]
SANDERSON, WILHELMINA, eldest daughter of William
  Sanderson a merchant in Edinburgh, married Auren Garrett
  a merchant in Peoria, Illinois, at George Callendar's house in
  Walnut Grove, Woodford County, Illinois, 20.2.1856.
  [CM#2-751]
SANDERSON, ..., daughter of David S. Sanderson and his wife
  ...... daughter of W.D.Scott in Edinburgh, born 27.1.1857 in
  Peoria, Illinois. [EEC#23108]
SCARTH, ROBERT, of Binscarth, married Jemima Eliza
  Stevenson, youngest daughter of James Stevenson in New
  Edinburgh, late of Leith, at Rideau Cottage, New Edinburgh,
  Canda West, 9.4.1855. [EEC.22732]
SCOBIE, NEIL FARQUHAR MACKINNON, Captain of the
  Highland Rifles, married Louisa Phoebe Sullivan, daughter
  of Dr Henry Sullivan, FRCSL, Toronto, there 24.8.1876
  [AJ#6715]
SCOBIE, NEIL F.M., in Hawkhill then in Canada, 7.11.1878.
  [SRO.RS.Fortrose#2/284]
SCOTT, JANET, relict of John Scott in Cupar, died in Fullarton,
  Ontario, 13.4.1875. [PJ]
SCOTT, WILLIAM JOHN, of Teviotbank, Roxburghshire, married
  Teresa Newcomen Harris, youngest daughter of John Harris
  RN, in London, Canada West, 18.8.1859. [EEC#23415]
SCOTT, WILLIAM, second son of Lieutenant Scott of the Fife
  Militia, died in Mobile, Alabama, 11.7.1860. [FH]

SAUNDERS, HENRY CHALMERS, born 1835, youngest son of
John S. Saunders, died in Fredericton, New Brunswick,
11.9.1856. [CM#20917]

SCOTT, ALEXANDER, second son of J. Scott a farmer from
Walton, Fife, died in Fullarton, Canada West, 25.3.1869.
[FH]

SCOTT, ALISON ERSKINE, youngest daughter of Ebenezer Scott
a surgeon in Dalkeith, married W.G.Adams, a merchant in
Memphis, USA, in Memphis 18.1.1839. [EEC#19874]

SCOTT, ARCHIBALD, born in Scotland 1795, a butcher, arrived in
Boston, Charlestown District, USA, late 1821 on the brig
Missionary, Captain Sears. [USNA]

SCOTT, HELEN, born 1780, from Paisley, wife of George
Carswell, died at Wing Lake, Bloomfield township, Oakland
County, Michigan, 28.8.1844. [SG#1342]

SCOTT, JAMES, from Collessie, Fife, died at Burnbrae, Seymour
East, by Belleville, Canada West, 27.1.1864. [FH]

SCOTT, JANE DALGLEISH, eldest daughter of W.D.Scott in
Edinburgh, married David T.N.Sanderson, at George
Callendar's house in Walnut Grove, Woodford County,
Illinois, 20.2.1856. [CM#20751]

SCOTT, JOAN, born 1872, daughter of Alexander Scott from
Leven, Fife, died in Cronly, North Carolina, 29.1.1885. [PJ]

SCOTT, JOHN, a farmer from Walton, Fife, died in Hamilton,
Canada West, 14.10.1851. [PJ]

SCOTT, JOHN, in Scarborough, Ontario, 4.9.1858.
[SRO.RS.Annan#10/152]

SCOTT, JOHN, born 1822, son of Thomas Scott innkeeper in
Pitlessie, Fife, died in Cleveland, Ohio, 25.1.1897. [FH]

SCOTT, PATRICK, born 1817, third son of William Scott in
Aberdeen, died in Detroit 13.9.1849. [AJ#5309]

SCOTT, PETER, a shoemaker in Toledo, Ohio, 6.9.1878.
[SRO.RS.Forfar#35/48]

SCOTT, THOMAS, paymaster of the 70th Regiment, brother of Sir
Walter Scott, 'he had been in Canada since the
commencement of the late American war serving with his
regiment', died in Quebec 14.2.1823. [DPCA#1329]

SCOTT, WILLIAM, a builder in Edinburgh then a master mason on
the Rideau Canal, died at Smith's Falls, Rideau Canal,
Upper Canada, 4.9.1831. [AJ#4377][EEC#18729]

SCOTT, Mrs WILLIAM, born 1812, from West Wemyss, Fife, died
at the house of her son-in-law Thomas Blyth in America
20.11.1889. [FFP]

SCOTT, ..., daughter of W.D.Scott in Edinburgh, wife of David S.
    Sanderson, died in Peoira, Illinois, 27.1.1857. [EEC#21036]
SCOUGALL, JANET, daughter of Richard Scougall in Leith,
    married Robert Henry Liston, manager of the Bank of British
    America in St John's, New Brunswick, in Manchester
    11.7.1837. [DPCA#1828]
SCOUGALL, RICHARD, late of Leith, died at his daughter Mrs
    Liston's house in Montreal 11.9.1841.
    [AJ#4892][EEC#20269]
SCRYMGEOUR, JAMES, from Edinburgh, died in New York
    12.5.1851. [W#1228]
SEATH, ROBERT, born in Cupar, emigrated to Montreal 1843, a
    merchant tailor, died in Montreal 10.9.1893. [FJ: 30.9.1893]
SEATH, THOMAS, born 1817, a builder from Cupar, died in
    Montreal 24.1.1863. [FA]
SEATH, WILLIAM, from Auchtermuchty, in Detroit, married Katie
    McKay, youngest daughter of John McKay in Grand Rapids,
    Michigan, there 28.11.1877. [PJ]
SELLAR, DAVID P., son of Patrick Sellar of Westfield, Moray,
    married Mary Van Horne Norrie, second daughter of A.
    Norrie of New York, there 3.12.1859.
    [EEC#23459][CM#21918]
SHADE, ABSOLOM, born 1793, died in Galt, Canada West,
    15.3.1862. [AJ#5962]
SHAW, DAVID, station master at Boat of Garten, then a farmer at
    Strone of Cally, Blairgowrie, Perthshire, later in Colorado,
    11.9.1871. [SRO.RS.Forfar#26/253]
SHAW, ELIZA MARY, daughter of Robert Shaw in Cupar, died in
    Toronto 16.2.1866. [FA]
SHAW, JANE, eldest daughter of Andrew Shaw, married Robert
    John Pilkington, royal military draughtsman, in Montreal
    30.1.1850. [W#1083]
SHAW, ..., daughter of James Shaw, born in Toronto 8.12.1847.
    [SG#1687]
SHEDDEN, ..., born 1811, second daughter of Thomas Shedden
    in Glasgow, wife of Charles Jackson, a Lieutenant of the US
    Navy, died in Middleton, Connecticut, 9.7.1833. [SG#185]
SHEED, GEORGE. a Presbyterian minister, died in Ancaster,
    Upper Canada, 26.11.1832. [AJ#4437]
SHEED, ROBERT, a merchant, died in Ancaster, Upper Canada,
    3.8.1832, and his wife Jean Leslie died there 6.8.1832.
    [AJ#4418]

SHEPHERD, HENRIETTA, wife of James Finlay, died at 107
Cathedral Street, Baltimore, 29.7.1871. [FH]

SHEPPARD, ROBERT, from Balmerino, died at West Madison
Street, Chicago, 4.2.1872. [PJ]

SHETKY, G., son of the late Mr Shetky, died in Philadelphia
11.12.1831. [EEC#18767]

SHEWAN, ALEXANDER, from St Fergus, Aberdeenshire,
educated at King's College, Aberdeen, graduated MA
3.1855, later a Professor in Montreal. [KCA#307]

SHIELLS, MARGARET, wife of Porterfield Howatt, from
Burntisland, died at Pine Point, Canada West, 26.7.1868.
[DP]

SHIER, JAMES, son of David Shier a land surveyor in Aberdeen,
educated at Marischal College, Aberdeen, graduated MA in
1849, later a schoolmaster in New Jersey. [MCA.II#547]

SHIREFFS, ANN, born 1800, wife of James Dow, died in Maryhill,
Woolwich, Canada West, 25.8.1848. [AJ#5257]

SIMPSON, AEMILIUS, Lieutenant RN, son of Alexander Simpson
in Dingwall, died at Ness Fort on the Simpson River on the
north west coast of America, 13.9.1831.
[AJ#4404][EEC#18876]

SIMPSON, ALEXANDER, late of Simpson and Kelso in Greenock,
died in New Orleans 5.4.1849. [SG#1820]

SIMPSON, ANDREW, born 1835, son of Andrew Simpson a
blacksmith in Auchtermuchty, died at his sister's residence in
Newburgh, South Cleveland, Ohio, 25.7.1881. [PJ]

SIMPSON, ..., son of George Simpson of La Chine, born in
Montreal 14.6.1850. [W#XI.1128]

SIMPSON, ..., son of Reverend George Simpson, born 31.7.1862
at the United Presbyterian Manse, Westminster, London,
Canada West. [AJ#5981]

SIMSON, DAVID, youngest son of James Simson a builder in
Cupar, Fife, died in St John's, New Brunswick, 26.7.1872.
[PJ]

SIMSON, JAMES, a merchant in Montreal, son of James Simson a
tenant in Posso, Peebles, died 7.3.1835. [AJ#4579]

SIMPSON, JOHN, late a farmer in Hayfield, Kirkcaldy, son of Peter
Simpson a tenant in Wester Gourdie, Dundee, died in New
York 23.12.1851. [FA:17.1.1852]

SIMPSON, WILLIAM, MD, born 1815, second son of John
Simpson a farmer in Boghead of Duniugas, Alvah, died at
Lexington College, Lexington, Kentucky, 9.4.1842.
[AJ#4936]

SIMPSON, WILLIAM, a druggist, formerly a precentor and teacher
of Sacred Music in Aberdeen, died in St John,
Newfoundland, 12.1.1844. [AJ#5063]

SINCLAIR, ALEXANDER, a merchant, formerly of Little Faudie,
Perthshire, sometime Adjutant of the Breadalbane
Fencibles, died in Charleston, South Carolina, 1.8.1838.
[SG#722]

SINCLAIR, BENJAMIN W., third son of Alexander Sinclair a
merchant in Thurso, married Susan, second daughter of
Major Faries of Savannah, in Savannah, North America,
24.11.1842. [AJ#4965]

SINCLAIR, MARGARET ELIZABETH, second daughter of John
Sinclair, Alfred Place, London, married Francis Voorhees in
New York 1847. [EEC#21481]

SKENE, CHARLOTTE, born 1847 eldest daughter of William
Skene a farmer in Banchory Tiernan, wife of J.C.Rawlins,
died in Pleasant Valley, Jo. Davies County, Illinois,
14.2.1876. [AJ#6689]

SKENE, GEORGE, born 1842, eldest son of William Skene from
Kineaky, Banchory-Tiernan, Aberdeenshire, died in
Savannah, Tennessee, 10.4.1862. [AJ#5969]

SKENE, JOHN DUNCAN, son of Thomas Skene the Inspector of
the Poor of Old Machar, educated at Marischal College,
Aberdeen, 1852, later a commission agent in San Francisco.
[MCA.II#559]

SKENE, WILLIAM, born 1805, eldest son of William Skene in
Leven, Fife, died in Charleston, South Carolina, 26.10.1841.
[FH:9.12.1841]

SKINNER, JOHN R., son of Andrew Skinner, Cupar Road,
Auchtermuchty, married Lucy Santoro, at Santoro House,
Cleveland, Ohio, 18.6.1884. [PJ]

SKINNER, Mrs MARY, born 1752, widow of Reverend Donald
Skinner in Ardnamurchan, died in Pictou, Nova Scotia, 1831.
[EEC#18635]

SKIRVING, ARCHIBALD, born 1800, from Wemyss, Fife, died in
Little Rock, Arkansas, 10.2.1875. [FFP]

SKIRVING, Mr ..., Forres, died in America 1833. [AJ#4482]

SKIRVING, JESSIE CARNEGIE, wife of Reverend Professor
Leach, Vice Principal of McGill College and minister of St
George's, died at McGill College, Montreal, 21.2.1848.
[EEC#21635][SG#1703]

SMART, ANN CHRISTIAN, daughter of James Smart and grand-
daughter of James Gray a writer in Cupar, died in Kansas
City 21.7.1877. [PJ]

SMART, ROBERT, born in St Monance, Fife, a seaman, died in
San Francisco 10.1849. [FJ,7.2.1850]

SMITH, Captain ALEXANDER, master of the <u>Charlotte of Belfast</u>,
late of Aberdeen, died in New Orleans, 10.3.1848.
[AJ#5233]

SMITH, BARBARA, wife of George Thomson a farmer from
Arneyburn, Auchterless, Aberdeenshire, died at Lake Simco,
Canada West, 27.1.1862. [AJ#5956]

SMITH, DANIEL, born 1799 in Aberdeen, died in Longueli,
Ottawa, 17.4.1848. [AJ#5237]

SMITH, GEORGE N., youngest son of William Smith a tailor in
Cupar, emigrated to St Stephen, New Brunswick, 1870, died
12.1883. [PJ: 9.2.1884]

SMITH, ISABEL GAIR ROSE, youngest daughter of Reverend
Robert Smith in Cromarty, married Reverend George
Romanes in Beckwith, Upper Canada, 12.8.1835. [AJ#4578]

SMITH, ISABELLA, daughter of George Smith in Aberdeen,
married Reverend George Milne MA a missionary of the
Society for the Propagation of the Gospel, in Quebec
Cathedral, 17.10.1842. [AJ#4950]

SMITH, JAMES, born 1775, late seedsman in Aberdeen, died in
Maryton, Brantford, Canada West, 12.6.1844. [AJ#5036]

SMITH, Reverend JAMES, late of the Secession Church, Nicolson
Place, Lauriston, and of Washington, Pennsylvania, died at
13 Surrey Street, Lauriston, Glasgow, 12.3.1845. [W#553]

SMITH, ..., son of James Smith in Mississippi, born at 23 Upper
Gray Street, Edinburgh, 19.3.1856. [CM#20744]

SMITH, JAMES HORNE, from Union City, Indiana, married Mary
Milne, eldest daughter of William Milne a farmer, at Perkhill,
Lumphanan, 31.3.1876. [AJ#6691]

SMITH, JAMES LEONARD, Glen Irvine, married Isabella Barker,
in Guelph, Upper Canada, 22.10.1844. [AJ#5059]

SMITH, JANE, wife of David Durie of Teasses, Fife, died at Ten
Park Lot, Sydenham, Owen Sound, Canada West,
28.3.1858. [FH]

SMITH, Dr JOHN, in Carolina, 1827. [SRO.RD5.332.220]

SMITH, Reverend JOHN, died in Beckwith, Upper Canada,
17.4.1851. [W#1222]

SMITH, JOHN, a hardware merchant in New Orleans, 13.2.1878.
[SRO.RS.Forfar#34/132]

SMITH, JOSEPH HARRIS, from Paisley, died in New Orleans
9.1850. [W#1205]

SMITH, ..., daughter of James Lamond Smith, born 13.10.1845 in
Lescraig, Canada West. [AJ#5108]

SMITH, MARGARET, born 1817, second daughter of John Smith
a writer in Huntley, and wife of Alexander Gordon, died in
Madoc, Upper Canada, 21.10.1848. [AJ#5264]

SMITH, MARY, Drummond Lodge, Callendar, Perthshire, only
daughter of Reverend James Smith minister of Ettrick,
married Peter William Wallace, MD, RN Hospital,
Esquimault, Vancouver Island, there 20.1.1862.
[EEC#23693]

SMITH, ROBERT, a merchant, third son of James Smith a farmer
in Dumpston, died in Laynesport, USA, 25.8.1849.
[AJ#5328]

SMITH, ROBERT, son of William Smith in Cupar, died on passage
from Jamaica to New York 21.4.1851. [FJ]

SMITH, WALTER, born 1853, eldest son of John Smith a
cabinetmaker from Teasses, Fife, died at Owen Sound,
Canada West, 28.3.1878. [FH]

SMITH, WILLIAM, a merchant, died in Montreal 18.10.1848.
[SG#1767]

SMITH, WILLIAM STEWART, LL.D., Principal of the High School,
Professor Elect of Classical Literature, at the Quebec Marine
College, died in Quebec 14.4.1862. [AJ#5966]

SMITH,......., son of William Smith of HM Customs, born in St
Johns, New Brunswick, 13.5.1851. [W#1224]

SOMERS, ANDREW, from St Monance, Fife, emigrated to
America 5.1852, landed there 7.1852. [PR,3.7.1852]

SOMERS, DAVID, from St Monance, Fife, emigrated to America
5.1852, landed there 7.1852. [PR,3.7.1852]

SOMERVILLE, ALEXANDER, son of Reverend Simon Somerville
in Elgin, died in Tuscombea, Alabama, 11.8.1838. [AJ#4737]

SOMMERVILLE, EMMA, wife of Alexander Sommerville, did in
Quebec 29.5.1859. [CM#21760]

SOMERVILLE, MARY, relict of Reverend William Horne,
Braehead, Lanarkshire, died in Yorktown, Delaware County,
Indiana, 15.4.1850. [W#XI.1110]

SOUTAR, JAMES WILLIAM, born 1823, youngest son of William
Soutar a farmer in Auchlin, died at his brother's house in
Sandusky, Ohio, 14.5.1849. [AJ#5293]

SOUTAR, ..., daughter of ... Soutar, born 19.11.1841 at the Manse of Newcastle, Miramachi, [AJ#4902]

SPARKES, ELLEN MARION, granddaughter of George Wilson a butcher in Cupar, married Charles F.W.Browne, in Kingston, Ontario, 5.3.1880. [PJ]

SPENCE, ALEXANDER, from Cupar, emigrated to America 2.1871. [PJ, 4.3.1871]

SPINK, CAROLINE, youngest daughter of Charles Spink of Eden Grove, wife of Joseph Marshal, died in Montreal 13.7.1843. [EEC#20670]

STARK, Reverend ANDREW, LLD, in New York, died in Dennyloanhead Manse 18.8.1849. [AJ#5308][SG#1858]

STARK, BARBARA, born 1814, a servant, died in an explosion on the Lady of the Lake near Quebec 7.9.1834. [AJ#4429]

STARK, JAMES, nephew of James Ferguson a manufacturer in Aberdeen, and for many years his agent in Halifax, Nova Scotia, died in Oregon Territory 6.1843. [AJ#5012]

STARK, ROBERT, chief engineer, eldest son of James Stark in Burntisland, died in Norfolk, USA, 9.3.1879. [PJ]

STEDMAN, ..., daughter of Hunter Stedman, born in Philadelphia, Nova Scotia, 19.7.1849. [SG#1847]

STEELE, DAVID HUTTON, second son of James Steele, 55 Nicolson Street, Edinburgh, grandson of David Hutton in Cupar, died in Sussex, New Brunswick, 13.7.1879. [FH]

STEEL, ELIZABETH, relict of Alexander Newlands, from Glasgow, died in Melbourne, Eastern Townships, Canada, 16.3.1851. [W#1205]

STEPHEN, ROBERT, born 1810, late a farmer in Balbridie, Durris, died in Knoxville, Knox County, Illinois, 4.3.1844. [AJ#5024]

STEPHEN, WILLIAM, born 1812, a merchant, died in Montreal 8.7.1862. [AJ#5978]

STEPHENSON, WILLIAM, born in Scotland 1793, a carpenter, arrived in New York on the ship Camillas, Captain Peck, 1821. [USNA]

STEVEN, JEMIMA STEWART, eldest daughter of William Steven late of Edinburgh, married John Young jr., a merchant, in Hamilton, Upper Canada, 5.4.1844. [W#5.454]

STEVEN, WILLIAM, late a hat manufacturer in Edinburgh, died in Hamilton, Canada, 5.3.1845. [EEC#211176][W#561]

STEVENSON, ISABELLA, born 1794, daughter of William Clarke late of Shutterflat, Beith, Ayrshire, died at Bankside, Scarboro, Canada West, 20.5.1848. [SG#1730]

STEVENSON, JANE, eldest daughter of Reverend David
Stevenson in Wilton, married James Favish, a merchant in
Montreal, at Wilton Manse 31.8.1840. [EEC#20098]

STEWART, CHARLES, from Forres, Morayshire, educated at
King's College, Aberdeen, graduated MA 3.1846, later a
merchant in America. [KCA#298]

STEWART, CHARLES, born 1794, formerly a merchant in
Aberdeen, died at Bear Creek, Upper Canada, 22.10.1861.
[AJ#5944]

STEWART, CHARLES, eldest son of John Stewart a gamekeeper
in Fordell, Fife, died in Brooklyn, New York, 12.2.1872. [DP]

STEWART, DOUGLAS, in Halifax, 1832. [SRO.RD5.460.469]

STEWART, JAMES, formerly a merchant in Newfoundland, then
Provost of Greenock, died 12.11.1837. [DPCA#1843]

STEWART, JANET, eldest daughter of James Stewart a vintner in
Glasgow, married Thomas Walker, in Philadelphia
24.5.1838. [SG#675]

STEWART, JOHN, in Quebec, 1837. [SRO.RD5.574.1]

STEWART, JOHN M.M., a law clerk in Osnaburg Street, Forfar,
then in Quednesset, East Greenwich, Rhode Island,
10.7.1871.[SRO.RS.Forfar#26/223]

STEWART, MARY AITKEN, infant daughter of David Stewart from
Cupar, died in San Francisco 23.1.1877. [PJ]

STEWART, MUNGO, son of Duncan Stewart in Pitlochry,
Perthshire, died at his brother's home in Zavala, Texas,
38.8.1876. [AJ#6715]

STEWART, MURDOCH, from Contin, educated at King's College,
Aberdeen, graduated MA 3.1834, later a minister in Nova
Scotia. [KCA#289]

STEWART, PETER, a merchant in Dalhousie, New Brunswick,
married Mary Hamilton, second daughter of John Hamilton a
merchant in Glasgow, at Govan Bank 1.4.1833.
[DPCA,12.4.1833]

STEWART, WALTER, a druggist and general merchant, West
River Street, Rhode Island, 20.8.1877.
[SRO.RS.Forfar#33/253]

STEWART, WILLIAM, in Upper Canada, 1836.
[SRO.RD5.564.634]

STEWART, WILLIAM L, Captain of the Royal Regiment, son of
Lieutenant Colonel Stewart, CB, HEICS, married Elizabeth
Sands Shore, daughter of George Shore, Rose Hall,
Fredericton, New Brunswick, in Fredericton 19.4.1849.
[EEC#21812]

STOBIE, KENNETH S., died in West Gwilliamsburg, York, Upper
Canada, 20.8.1834. [AJ#4429]

STOBIE, MACKAY JOHN, died in York, Upper Canada,
20.8.1834. [AJ#4429]

STRACHAN, JOHN, born 1763, Campfield, Kincardine O'Neil,
Aberdeenshire, emigrated to America 1819, died in
Waterford, New York, 1850. [AJ#5340]

STRACHAN, ROBERT M., born in Strathmiglo, Fife, died in New
York 16.4.1862. [FA]

STRATTON, ..., son of Dr Stratton surgeon in the Royal Navy,
born in Montreal 8.2.1849. [EEC#21781]

STRATTON, WALLACE, infant son of Dr Stratton RN, died in
Charlottetown, Prince Edward Island, 2.3.1855. [EEC'22718]

STRONACH, ISABELLA, relict of James Watkins a merchant from
Aberdeen, died at 470 15th Street, Detroit, Michigan,
21.3.1876. [AJ#6691]

STUART, CHARLES, born 1797, son of Professor Stuart in
Aberdeen, a merchant in Quebec, died there 13.12.1848.
[AJ#5270][SG#1785]

STUART, DAVID KNOX, son of John Stuart of East Kilbride, died
in New Orleans 10.4.1851. [W#1248]

STUART, JOHN FISH, born 1821, second son of Robert Stuart,
Gortinean House, Killean, Argyll, died in Kingston, Canada,
2.9.1844. [SG#1347][W#5.515]

STUART, PETER, a printer from Peterhead, Aberdeenshire, died
in Augusta, Georgia, 16.6.1862. [AJ#5996]

SUTHERLAND, ALEXANDER, formerly a druggist in Aberdeen,
then of Millar and Company Druggists in New York, died in
New York 12.7.1846. [AJ#5143]

SUTHERLAND, ALEXANDER, born in Edinburgh, died in Mobile,
Alabama, 26.1.1857. [EEC#21055]

SUTHERLAND, DANIEL, born 1782, late printer in the King's
Printing Office in Edinburgh, died in Montreal 23.8.1846.
[AJ#5150]

SUTHERLAND, JOHN, born 1818, son of William Sutherland a
fisheries officer in Cullen, a merchant in New York, died at
359 6th Avenue, New York, 25.7.1861. [AJ#5927]

SUTHERLAND, SAMUEL, son of Thomas Erskine Sutherland a
merchant in Edinburgh, died in Vandreal, Canada,
25.10.1848. [SG#1795]

SUTHERLAND, THOMAS, born 1772, from Edinburgh, died at
Moore River, St Clair, Canada West, 16.2.1850.
[W#XI.1098]

SUTTIE, MARGARET, born in Brunton, Fife, 1831, wife of Charles
Reekie from Carphin, died at 56 10th Street, Hoboken, New
Jersey, 15.18.1874. [PJ]

SWAN, MARY ANN, born in Scotland 1797, with children, arrived
in New York on the ship Camillas, Captain Peck, 1821.
[USNA]

SWAN, THOMAS, born 1802, a farmer formerly a dairyman in
Cumberland Street, Edinburgh, died at York Mills, York
township, Canada West, 8.2.1862. [EEC#23690]

SYME, JAMES, in Glasgow then in Boston, USA, 2.12.1856.
[SRO.RS.Forfar#18/146]

TAILYOUR, WILLIAM RENNY, born 1814, son of Alexander R.
Tailyour of Borrowfield, died in Fergus, Upper Canada,
14.10.1839. [EEC#19987]

TAIT, MARGARET, eldest daughter of William Tait a merchant,
married Reverend John Mackinnon Hopewell, from Nova
Scotia, in Edinburgh 2.8.1859. [CM#21796]

TAIT, ROBERT, in Elizabethtown, North Carolina, married Miss
E.B.Vert, both from Haddington, Scotland, in New York
17.2.1855. [EEC#22710]

TAIT, WILLIAM, born 1809, a surgeon, son of James Tait in
Newton Stewart, died in Quebec 14.6.1832. [FH#543]

TARBAT, ALEXANDER, a plasterer in Forfar, Angus, then in New
York 26.5.1857. [SRO.RS.Forfar#18/206]

TAYLOR, ALEXANDER, born 1804, commander of the ship
Magistrate, drowned off Savanna 15.9.1837. [DPCA#1839]

TAYLOR, ALICE CHARLOTTE, wife of George Taylor of the 93rd
Highlanders, died in Montreal 20.3.1845. [AJ#5076]

TAYLOR, GEORGE, born 1802, late of the Mill of Inchmario,
Upper Banchory, died in Detroit, Michigan, 9.7.1849.
[AJ#5303]

TAYLOR, GEORGE CAVENDISH, late of the 95th Regiment of
Foot, married Louisa Carroll, second daughter of Colonel
Charles Carroll in Maryland, and great granddaughter of
Charles Carroll of Carrollton the last surviving signer of the
Declaration of Independence, in Baltimore 28.12.1858.
[CM#21635]

SUTHERLAND, GEORGE, born 1825, from Ross-shire, died at
    Owen Sound, Canada, 1.1.1857. [EEC#21007]
TAYLOR, GEORGE CHARLES, infant son of George Taylor of the
    93rd Highlanders, died in Montreal 14.4.1845. [AJ#5081]
TAYLOR, INNES MUNRO, son of R. Sutherland Taylor, Weston
    House, Cupar, Fife, married Susannah Margaret Fraser,
    youngest daughter of J.R.Fraser, in Montreal 25.1.1868. [FJ]
TAYLOR, Mrs JANE, eldest daughter of John Ritchie in Byers of
    Balmerino, Fife, died in Freeport, Pennsylvania, 9.2.1888.
    [PJ]
TAYLOR, JANETTE, born in Dumfries 1776, a niece of John Paul
    Jones, emigrated to USA 1828, died in New York 5.3.1844.
    [AJ#5021][EEC#20013]
TAYLOR, JOHN, a merchant in New York, died there 1.4.1840.
    [EEC#20052]
TAYLOR, JOHN, born 1768, died in Westmoreland, Cheraw,
    South Carolina, 20.10.1848. [SG#1768]
TAYLOR, MARY, youngest daughter of Matthew Taylor, married
    James Wiggins, a merchant in New York, in Glasgow
    16.9.1857. [EEC#21210]
TAYLOR, THOMAS WARDLAW, MA, barrister at law, married
    Jessie Cameron, eldest daughter of John Cameron, in
    Toronto 8.12.1858. [CM#21613]
TAYLOR, WILLIAM, late a farmer at Thomastown, Drumblade,
    died on passage from New Orleans to St Louis 30.3.1842.
    [AJ#4926]
TAYLOR, WILLIAM ROSS, infant son of Dr Taylor, Deputy
    Inspector General of Hospitals, died in Toronto 13.6.1862.
    [AJ#5974]
TAYLOR, ..., daughter of T.W.Taylor a barrister at law, born in
    Toronto 30.10.1859. [CM#21885]
TAYLOR, ..., son of Alexander Taylor, born near York, Grand
    River, Canada West, 1859. [CM#21872]
TEESDALE, JOHN, from Larkhall, Lanarkshire, settled in
    Philadelphia by 1848. [SRO.RH1.2.704]
TELFER, ELIZABETH, widow of ... Reid a saddler in Ayr, died in
    Montreal 11.8.1832. [AJ#4422]
TEMPLE, JAMES, born 1822, fourth son of Robert Temple in
    Cloisterseat, Udny, Aberdeenshire, died in Port Dover,
    Upper Canada, 26.12.1845. [AJ#5120]
THAIN, MARY EVERETTA, second daughter of Thomas Thain in
    Montreal, died in Canterbury 22.10.1843. [AJ#4999]

THOM, ..., son of Adam Thom LL.D., Chief Resident Judge of the Hudson Bay Company, born at the Fort, Red River, 2.8.1843. [AJ#5001]

THOMS, ..., daughter of William Thoms from Edinburgh, born in Yorkville, New York, 28.2.1852. [FJ#1005]

THOMSON, AGNES, daughter of George Thomson in America, wife of William Alexander in Cockenzie, died in Tranent 26.1.1848. [SG#1686]

THOMSON, AGNES, daughter of Robert Thomson a builder in Gladney, Ceres, Fife, married Andrew Forrester a flax manufacturere in Mitchell, at Toronto 14.10.1870. [FH]

THOMSON, ANDREW, of Kinloch, WS, died in Easton, Saratoga, New York, 19.8.1831. [AJ#4369][EEC#18705]

THOMSON, CHARLOTTE CADDY, wife of John Carnegie, died in Edrom, Peterboro, Upper Canada, 7.3.1859. [EEC#23344]

THOMSON, GEORGE, a teacher, late of the Free Church School in Kintore, Aberdeenshire, died in Chatham, Canada West, 27.4.1862. [AJ#5967]

THOMSON, GEORGE, a merchant, fourth son of James Thomson a writer in Cupar, died in New York 2.8.1864. [FA]

THOMSON, JAMES, his wife and 2 daughters, from Morayshire, died in America 1833. [AJ#4482]

THOMSON, JESSIE, daughter of Alexander Thomson from Leven, Fife, died in Hoboken, New Jersey, 26.8.1873. [FFP]

THOMPSON, J.R., of Brock, a solicitor, married Jean Johnson, second daughter of Captain William Johnson RN of Georgina, Lake Simcoe, Upper Canada, at Toronto 16.9.1852. [W#1375]

THOMSON, JOHN, fourth son of John Thomson a manufacturer in Strathmiglo, Fife, married Aggie Larkin of Cheyne, in Cheyne, Wyoming, 23.9.1885. [FH]

THOMSON, PATRICK BAKER, in Quebec, 1831. [SRO.RD5.433.189]

THOMSON, ROBERT, born 1832, from Buckhaven, Fife, died in Detroit 7.11.1908. [FH]

TILLOCH, ELIZABETH, daughter of Alexander Tilloch LL.D., relict of John Galt, died in Sherbrooke, Canada West, 6.11.1851. [W#1283]

TODD, JOHN, born in Glasgow 1793, to Hudson Bay on the Edward and Anne 1811, Hudson Bay Company employee 1811-1852, later settled at Oak Bay, Victoria, British Columbia. [HBRS.3.461]

TODD, JOHN, sr., born in Anstruther 1807, died in Brooklyn, New
    York, 6.3.1877. [EFR]
TODD, HENRY, second son of Richard Todd in Balcomie, Fife,
    died in Boston, Massachusetts, 25.12.1852. [FH]
TORRANCE, ELLIOT, wife of Alexander T. Galt, died in
    Sherbrooke, Canada, 24.5.1850. [W#XI.1124]
TOVEY, JOHN, in Quebec, 1830. [SRO.RD5.425.563]
TULLOCH, JOHN THOMAS, from Badcall, son of Reverend
    George Tulloch in Edrachillis, educated at Marischal
    College, Aberdeen, 1859, later in British Columbia.
    [MCA.II#585]
TURNBULL, ROBERT WILSON, youngest son of James Walter
    Turnbull a draper in Jedburgh, died in New York 5.1.1840.
    [EEC#20014]
TURNER, CATHERINE AITKEN, wife of John George MacTavish
    of the Hudson Bay Company, died in Montreal 8.10.1841.
    [AJ#4895]
TYNLING, MARY, wife of Thomas Cattenach a builder late of
    Newcastle, died in Raleigh, North Carolina, 6.6.1839.
    [EEC#19993]
URE, JANET, daughter of William Ure in Glasgow, married James
    Scott of Montreal, in Glasgow 12.4.1831. [FH#476]
URE, LILLIAS, daughter of William Ure in Glasgow, married
    William Smith of Montreal, in Glasgow 12.4.1831. [FH#476]
URQUHART, DONALD, late of Dingwall, Ross-shire, married
    Catherine Bryant in Kingston, Canada, 20.12.1834.
    [AJ#4545]
URQUHART, WILLIAM D., MD, born in Aberdeen, member of the
    medical staff of the Emigrants Hospital, on Wards Island,
    New York, died there 28.12.1849. [AJ#5325]
WALKER, CHRISTIAN, wife of Thomas Logan jr., died in Jersey
    City, USA, 4.8.1849. [SG#1850]
WALKER, ELIZABETH, born 1817, daughter of William Walker in
    Luthrie, Fife, wife of James L. Main, died at Little Falls,
    Minneapolis, 1.2.1889. [PJ]
WALKER, GEORGE C., son of Gabriel Walker, died in New
    Orleans 18.8.1851. [W#11260]
WALKER, MAGGIE R., daughter of Isaac Walker a gamekeeper at
    Tarvit, Fife, married Henry Lister, a glover, in Scranton,
    Pennsylvania, 31.1.1870. [FH]
WALKER, MARGARET, eldest daughter of John Walker a leather
    merchant in St Andrews, died in New York 30.8.1849.
    [SG#1857]

WALKER, NEIL, born in Leven, Fife, married Barbara Murray in Leven 13.1.1821, emigrated to USA 1844, settled in Frye village, Andover, Massachusetts. [PJ, 4.3.1871]

WALKER, W., a banker, second son of A. Walker a leather merchant in Cupar, died in New York 15.9.1853. [FH]

WALKER, WILLIAM S., 86 Myrtle Avenue, Brooklyn, New York, 30.9.1852. [SRO.RS.Whithorn#3/107]

WALLACE, ANDREW, son of Andrew Wallace a farmer in Blairgreen, Fife, died at Whitehills, Oakland County, Michigan, 30.12.1842. [FH:9.3.1842]

WALLACE, ARCHIBALD, a writer from St Andrews, Fife, died in Quebec 21.6.1832. [FH:23.8.1832]

WALLACE, DANIEL, born 1874, son of George Wallace from Craigrothie, Fife, died at Clam Lake City, Michigan, 15.8.1875. [PJ]

WALLACE, HELEN, fifth daughter of William Wallace a merchant in Richmond, Virginia, grand-daughter of William Wallace a merchant in Peterhead, died in Richmond, Virginia, 31.9.1861. [AJ#5934]

WALLACE, MARGARET PORTER, daughter of Peter Wallace, former manager of the Royal Coachworks in Perth, married William Austen, an engineer, in Toronto 19.11.1859. [CM#21908]

WALLS, JOHN, born 1840, son of John Walls {died 1885} a farmer at Grange, and Janet Tosh {died 1873}, emigrated to Canada 3.1865, died in San Francisco 18.10.1885. [FFP, 23.3.1865]

WALLS, MARGARET, born 1817 in Beath, Fife, wife of Alexander Scott, died in Toronto 1.9.1887. [FFP]

WARDLAW, MARION A., died in Toronto 12.1.1855. [FJ]

WARRACK, CAROLINE, born 1859, youngest daughter of Alexander Warrack, died in Brooklyn, New York, 30.4.1862. [AJ#5967]

WATERS, ANN, eldest daughter of David Waters in Brems, Caithness, wife of Reverend David Sutherland a Congregationalist minister, died in Bath, New Hampshire, 3.3.1852. [W#1309]

WATERS, JAMES, born 1738 in America, married Mary MacMorland aged 35, in Kirkoswald, Ayrshire, 27.10.1837. [DPCA#1844]

WATSON, JAMES, son of James Watson WS, died in Toronto 9.4.1845. [EEC#21191]

WATSON, JAMES, son of Robert Watson, died in Detroit,
Michigan, 24.1.1848. [AJ#5285]

WATSON, JAMES, son of James Watson cashier of the Union
Bank in Glasgow, married Helen Dewar, eldest daughter of
Plummer Dewar, at Sandyford Place, Hamilton, Canada
West, 9.6.1859. [CM#21767]

WATSON, JOHN COOPER, 11 month old infant son of William
Wilson late a bookseller in Glasgow, died at sea off the
Banks of Newfoundland 2.7.1844. [SG#1324]

WATSON, MARION, wife of Reverend William Dickson, did in
Thorald, Canada West, 24.4.1859. [CM#21729]

WATSON, ROBERT, late a builder in Edinburgh, died in Errol,
Kent County, Upper Canada, 9.5.1846. [AJ#5138]

WATSON, ROBERT, late of Stoneywood, died in Detroit,
Michigan, 11.3.1848. [AJ#5285]

WATSON, ROBERT SCOTT, born in Anstruther 1861, second son
of Alexander Watson a shipbuilder, died at MacAulay's
Point, British Columbia, 28.8.1883. [EEC:9.11.1883]

WATSON, WILLIAM, an accountant with the Bank of British North
America in Montreal, eldest son of Archibald Watson in
Edinburgh, married Louisa Mathews Goodhue, eldest
daughter of George J. Goodhue a member of the Legislative
Council of Canada, in London, Canada West, 23.10.1856.
[CM#20944]

WATSON, ..., daughter of Walter Watson, manager of the Bank
of British North America in London, Canada West, there
9.9.1859. [EEC#23422]

WATT, CHARLES, born in Montrose 1752, to New Brunswick in
1780s with Captain Campbell's company of the 74th
Regiment under Colonel Abercrombie, died in Portland, New
Brunswick, 29.12.1841. [AJ#4911]

WEBSTER, JAMES, Fergus, Upper Canada, second son of
James Webster of Balruddery, Perthshire, married Margaret,
eldest daughter of George Wilson, Harvey Cottage, Nichol
township, Upper Canada, 6.3.1838. [AJ#4714]

WEBSTER, ..., daughter of James Webster, born in Fergus, Upper
Canada, 25.4.1842. [AJ#4928]

WEBSTER, ..., son of James Webster, county registrar, born in
Guelph, Canada West, 29.5.1861. [AJ#5920]

WEIR, GEORGE, from Aberlour, Banffshire, educated at King's
College, Aberdeen, graduated MA 3.1848, later Professor of
Classics in Kingston, Quebec. [KCA#300]

WEIR, ..., daughter of Deputy Commissary General Weir, born in Halifax, Nova Scotia, 8.1.1857.[EEC#21035]

WELSH, Mrs J., in New York, 1830. [SRO.RD5.418.689]

WESTON, ALICE ANNE, youngest child of Dr Paul Weston in Charleston, South Carolina, married Edward Mahon Roose, son of Sir David Roose, in Portobello 29.4.1842. [EEC#20357]

WESTON, ANTONIA BATTY, relict of Paul Weston MD, Charleston, South Carolina, died at 4 Windsor Terrace, Portobello, 16.12.1857. [EEC#21289]

WESTON, MARY ANN MAZYCK, second daughter of Paul Weston a physician in Charleston, South Carolina, married John Gibson WS, in Portobello 10.4.1849.

WESTWOOD, CATHERINE, third daughter of Hugh Westwood in Torryburn, Fife, married Robert Thomson, in Portland, Maine, 10.3.1870. [DP]

WHYTE, AGNES, born 1818 daughter of Joseph Whyte a surgeon late of Banff, wife of J. Whyte, died at 43 Queen Street, Charleston, South Carolina, 1842; mother of a son born 29.7.1842. [AJ#4940]

WHYTE, AGNES BRYSON, third daughter of Robert Whyte a merchant in Edinburgh, married James Sneddon, a civil engineer in Macon, Georgia, in New York 14.12.1851. [W#1279]

WHYTE, HELEN, eldest daughter of Reverend James Whyte in New York, died in Telford Street, Inverness, 1.1.1844. [AJ#5019]

WHITE, JOHN C, born in Abercrombie, Fife, 1800, '50 years in Montreal', died there 14.12.1885. [PJ]

WHITEHEAD, ELIZABETH, born 1856, from Edinburgh, wife of Reverend Daniel Anderson a missionary of the Free Church of Scotland, died in Brock, Canada West, 5.11.1858. [CM#21617]

WILKIE, THOMAS, born 1825, a stonemason from Strathmiglo, Fife, son of Thomas Wilkie (died 1827) and Margaret Kay (died 1859), emigrated to USA 1884, settled in Eau Claire, Wisconsin, died there 29.6.1899. [PJ]

WILKIE, THOMAS, born 1849, eldest son of Thomas Wilkie from Strathmiglo, Fife, killed in Eau Claire, Wisconsin, 7.1.1884. [PJ]

WILKIE, Mrs, born 1777, relict of Reverend Dr Wilkie of Quebec, died in Montreal 28.3.1852. [W#1325]

WILKINS, SARAH, born 1770, relict of Judge Wilkins of the Nova
Scotia Supreme Court, died in Windsor, Nova Scotia,
3.11.1859. [CM#21907]

WILLIAMSON, BENJAMIN, eldest son of Captain Williamson of 5
Raeburn Place, Edinburgh, died in New Orleans 4.1841.
[EEC#20224]

WILLIAMSON, DAVID, in Canada, 1850. [SRO.RD5.856.644]

WILLIAMSON, JAMES S., born in Cowdenbeath, married Annie E.
Todd daughter of Samuel A. Todd, in St Louis 1.1883. [PJ,
10.2.1883]

WILLIAMSON, ..., son of Mr Williamson, born in Kingston,
Canada West, 27.3.1847. [EEC#21494]

WILSON, ANN, eldest daughter of Thomas Wilson a carpenter in
St Monance, Fife, married Thomas Dodds of HM Naval
Yard, in Victoria, Vancouver, 20.11.1866. [FA]

WILSON, CHARLES, from Cowdenbeath, married Charlotte Robb,
second daughter of Alexander Robb in Cowdenbeath, at
Lilly, Cambric County, Pennsylvania, 6.2.1883. [FFP]

WILSON, JAMES, born 1822, from Lesliehead, Burntisland, died
in London, Ontario, 2.5.1898. [PJ]

WILSON, JOHN, MD of the 71st Light Infantry, died in Montreal
1843. [SG#1231]

WILSON, ROBERT, born 1846, third son of David Wilson in
Cowdenbeath, died in Brooklyn, New York, 1909. [DJ,
6.11.1909]

WILSON, WILLIAM, a merchant, died in New York 13.7.1844.
[SG#1322]

WISHART, WILLIAM, a shoemaker recently from Scotland, died in
Quebec 9.7.1832. [AJ#4422]

WISHART, Reverend WILLIAM T., minister of the Presbyterian
Church in Shelbourne, married Isabella, eldest daughter of
John Morton of Cornwallis, at Cornwallis, Nova Scotia,
19.9.1839. [SG#821]

WOOD, GEORGE, eldest son of Lord Wood, married Emma,
eldest daughter of Bernard Henry in Philadelphia, there
17.4.1845. [EEC#21191][W#571]

WOOD, JOHN, Slamannan, Stirlingshire, married Janet Hepburn,
younger daughter of John Hepburn, in Whitby, Canada
West, 18.3.1857. [EEC#21078]

WOOD, JOHN GILLESPIE, MD, married Harriet, fourth daughter
of John Johnston, at Isle aux Noix, Canada, 3.5.1841.
[AJ#4877]

WOOD, ..., son of Dr J.G.Wood, second class staff surgeon, born in Kingston, Canada, 30.10.1851. [W#1276]

WOOD, JAMES, born in Scotland 1776, a merchant, arrived in Savannah, USA, on the ship <u>Pallas</u>, Captain Land, late 1821. [USNA]

WOOD, MARY EMILY, born 1847, daughter of George Wood, died in Philadelphia 21.1.1850. [W#XI.1082]

WOODS, ELIZA G., youngest daughter of John Woods in Glasgow, married Alfred Pell, in New York 17.2.1848. [SG#1699]

WOODS, MARGARET, wife of Laurence Kidd, formerly of Kilmarnock, died in Canada 23.7.1832. [AJ#4422]

WRIGHT, PATRICK R., from Aberdeen, married Mary Anne, only daughter of William Chapman from Yorkshire, in Coburg, Canada, 4.3.1846. [AJ#5133]

WYLLIE, CHRISTINA, wife of Reverend James Harper, died in Ellicot, Baltimore, USA, 15.11.1838. [SG#726]

WYLLIE, ELIZA, daughter of Peter Wyllie, emigrated via Glasgow on the <u>City of Glasgow</u> to New York bound for Boston, 18.6.1853. [FA, 25.6.1853]

WYLIE, JAMES, in Toledo, America, second son of Alexander Wylie a distiller in Campbelltown, Argyll, married Jane Greenlees, eldest daughter of William Greenlees, farmer in Ardnacross, Argyll, at Haarlem, Winnebago County, Illinois, 18.12.1851. [W#1301]

WYLLIE, JESSIE, eldest daughter of James Wyllie in Burnside, married Reverend Colin Campbell, Brockville, Upper Canada, at Burnside Ramsay 3.2.1838. [AJ#4702]

WYLLIE, JOHN, a glover in Orleans, Vermont, 15.11.1864. [SRO.RS.Whithorn#4/35, 43]

YOOL, JAMES, an engineer from Ceres, Fife, married Margaret Cameron Murray, youngest daughter of John Murray from Rothesay, in San Francisco 24.12.1883. [PJ]

YOUNG, GEORGE, born 1835, from Aberdeen, died in Montreal 13.3.1861. [AJ#5909]

YOUNG, HUGH, a merchant, second son of James Young the sheriff substitute of Kincardineshire, died in New Orleans 15.2.1833. [AJ#4449]

YOUNG, JAMES, son of Lieutenant George Young RN in Portsoy, died in St Louis, USA, 9.12.1848. [AJ#5276]

YOUNG, JOHN, of Culimore, Stirling, Judge of the 10th Judicial District of Pennsylvania, died in Greensburgh, Pennsylvania, 6.10.1840. [FH#995][AJ#4865]

YOUNG, JOHN, born 1843, fourth son of John Young late in
 Anstruther, died in Moville, USA, 17.9.1873. [EFR]

YOUNG, THOMAS, son of Archibald Young a farmer in Ingliston,
 died in New York 1.9.1844. [EEC#21093]

YOUNG, ..., son of William A.G.Young, born in Rosebank,
 Equimault, Vancouver Island, 27.1.1857.[EEC#23348]

YOUNGER, JAMES, born 1844 in Ceres, Fife, a shipbuilder,
 settled in Philadelphia 1872, died there 27.4.1894. [FH:
 16.5.1894]

YUILLE, GAVIN, born in Scotland, an Alderman of Mobile, died
 there 17.9.1849. [SG#1867]